Understanding Transitions in the Early Years

There are many transitions that children experience before they are five, including the first major transition from home to an early years setting. Successive changes can have a serious impact on young children and stress, separation and insecure attachments can affect not only a child's emotional health but also cognitive and intellectual development.

Understanding Transitions in the Early Years explains why transitions matter and provides practical guidance on how to support young children's developing emotional resilience and equip them to embrace change in the future. Aimed at practitioners and students, the book:

- draws together evidence from neuroscience, attachment theory, child development and childcare practices;
- provides a context for practitioners to empathise with children and families as they relate to their own understanding of the impact of change and transition;
- looks at ways to reduce the number of transitions including the key person approach;
- offers guidance and practical strategies for practitioners, managers and head teachers for supporting children through transitions.

Including case studies, examples of good practice and questions for reflection, this thought-provoking text emphasises the little things that practitioners can do for the individual children in their care to help them feel secure and confident when dealing with change.

Anne O'Connor is an Early Years Consultant. She has authored numerous articles for *Nursery World* including 'All About Transitions' which was included in the resource materials for the Early Years Foundation Stage (EYFS (2008)).

Understanding Transitions in the Early Years

Supporting change through attachment and resilience

Anne O'Connor

Routledge
Taylor & Francis Group

LONDON AND NEW YORK

2011001392

First published 2013
by Routledge
2 Park Square, Milton Park, Abingdon, Oxon OX14 4RN

Simultaneously published in the USA and Canada
by Routledge
711 Third Avenue, New York, NY 10017

Routledge is an imprint of the Taylor & Francis Group, an informa business

British Library Cataloguing in Publication Data
A catalogue record for this book is available from the British Library

Library of Congress Cataloging in Publication Data
O'Connor, Anne, 1957–
   Understanding transitions in the early years: supporting change through
   attachment and resilience/Anne O'Connor.
   p. cm.
   Includes bibliographical references and index.
   1. Attachment behavior in children. 2. Adjustment (Psychology) in
   children. 3. Security (Psychology) in children. 4. Child development.
   I. Title.
   BF723.A75O36 2012
   155.42'382–dc23   2012012767

ISBN: 978–0–415–59857–6 (hbk)
ISBN: 978–0–415–59858–3 (pbk)
ISBN: 978–0–203–11777–4 (ebk)

Typeset in Bembo and Helvetica Neue
by Florence Production Ltd, Stoodleigh, Devon

MIX
Paper from
responsible sources
FSC® C004839

Printed and bound in Great Britain by the MPG Books Group

For my son, Danny
and
in memory of my parents

2011001392

Contents

Acknowledgements

Thank you to the many people who assisted with information and examples used in the book: Nicola Crossland, Ruth Miller, Della Clark, Mia Clark and Tricia Carroll; Amanda Sinker and Liz Tattersall at Ridge County Primary School, Lancaster; Louise McCabe at Rising Stars Nursery and staff at Firbank Children's Centre, Lancaster; Angela Benson at Westgate Primary School and Children's Centre, Morecambe; Fran Butler and Sheena Wright from Devon County Council; Julie White of Bents Farm Nursery, Halifax.

I am very grateful for the support of the many friends and family who played their part in helping this book reach completion. Emma Aylett, Karen Allan, Gwen Atkinson, Vanessa Card, Della Clark, Gina Dowding, Mary and Marcel Driver and family, Inda Kaur, Jennifer Lauruol, Natasa Magdalenic-Bantic, Thomas and Alex O'Connor, Sam Riches and the Carroll-Webster family all provided encouragement through their gentle enquiries about the current stage of development, the provision of quiet spaces to write in and hearty reminders to crack on with it! Thanks go to Sue Gott for useful references, in-depth analysis of attachment theory and critical reflection as the chapters saw the light of day. Marion Russell and Bill Roberts provided valuable online support and knowledgeable first-hand perspectives on attachment and neuroscience. Thank you to the children, families and staff of Harbinger Early Years Unit in Tower Hamlets 1990–2000 who gave me such valuable insights into what really matters in the early years.

I am indebted to Wendy Scott, Julie Fisher, Richard Bowlby, Maria Robinson and Dorothy Y. Selleck for the inspiration behind much of the book and their generosity in discussing aspects of it with me. I want to thank Denise Bailey and Carlene Hutchinson for still being here after all these years, and to Danny I give my love and gratitude for teaching me everything I know about attachment, emotional resilience and living through transitions.

Sections of the book have also been informed by a five-part series written for *Nursery World* entitled 'Positive Relationships: Attachment', which ran from October 2007 to February 2008, and from an article entitled 'All About Transitions' (2006). I am very grateful to *Nursery World* for permission to use this material.

Introduction

The thing is . . . you just want to know will they love them as much as we do.

This was the comment made to me by a mother when I asked how she felt about her four-year-old daughter's first few days at school. The child seemed happy enough and all was going well, but in a few words this mother summed up the monumental – but mostly unspoken – concern that is probably at the heart of every parent's anxiety as they hand their precious babies (in school uniform) into the care of someone else.

There are all sorts of questions parents are supposed to ask of the school (or childcare) that they so carefully choose for their children. What is the behaviour policy? What Ofsted grading does it have? How good is the maths teaching?

'How well they will be loved?' isn't usually on the list. But perhaps it should be.

There is a wealth of material addressing the issues of transitions for young children, many of them referenced here. We are well aware that there are difficulties to overcome when children move from home, into daycare and education outside the home. We know that children's learning sometimes seems to regress when they move within settings or from class to class in the primary school. We know that some children need more help than others to 'cope' with transitions and separations – and that some of them get very anxious. We talk about 'smoothing' transitions and are urged to make them 'seamless' for children, whilst at the same time making the most of the learning and progression stimulated and provoked by new experiences.

The Centre for Excellence and Outcomes in Children and Young People's Services (C4EO) has produced a very useful review of all the research relating to educational transition from the early years through to post-16. The document has a long title but it's one that sums up what all of us, parents, practitioners and politicians, desire for our children: *Ensuring that all children and young people make sustained progress and remain fully engaged through all transitions between key stages* (C4EO: 2010). The document reviews all the main findings of research into educational transitions from the UK and beyond and highlights areas where further research is needed.

Most parents and early years practitioners will probably not be surprised to learn that:

- Children with more severe learning difficulties are likely to struggle with transition (Carlson et al. 2009).

- Children with low self-esteem or poor confidence may be more vulnerable at times of transition due to a lack of skills relating to emotional resilience (Working with Men 2004; Evangelou et al. 2008).

- Children who are youngest in their age group (often referred to as 'summer born' children) can be at a disadvantage during early years transitions. This might be because of relative immaturity/unsuitable environments/developmentally inappropriate expectations (Sanders et al. 2005; Crawford et al. 2007) though the extent of the difference in attainment seems to decrease in transitions beyond the age of compulsory schooling (Crawford et al. 2007; Sharp et al. 2009).

- There seems to be a relationship between socio-economic deprivation and poor experiences of transition. This could be linked to poor opportunities to socialise and regulate emotions (Miller et al. 2003; McIntyre et al. 2007; LoCasale-Crouch et al. 2008; Carlson et al. 2009).

- The support of friends and friendship groups helps protect children from the impact of transition (Sanders et al. 2005).

- Some children worry about transition and are anxious about the uncertainty of change: making new friends; understanding the rules; working with new teachers and a harder curriculum (Galton et al. 2003; Sanders et al. 2005; Merry 2007; Evangelou et al. 2008; Shields 2009).

- The degree of discontinuity between the curriculum and pedagogy of their old and new environments increases transition difficulty, particularly if there is insufficient collaboration between the two (Sanders et al. 2005; Stormont et al. 2005; McIntyre et al. 2007; Merry 2007; Centre for Community Health 2008; Shields 2009).

- This causes difficulties for parents as well as children (Shields 2009; C4EO 2010:19–24).

The review suggests there is clear evidence that 'transition poses a potential risk to the well being and progress of children and young people' (CE40 2010:34) and of an association between difficulties with educational transition and

- lower levels of attainment
- less positive attitudes to education and learning
- disengagement from education.

Asked originally, a few years ago, to write an extended article for *Nursery World* about transitions, I read everything I could on the subject, absorbed the research findings and the information about transition theory and handling change, and found myself looking for the 'love' in the accounts of children moving from home to daycare, from the '2–3s' room into '3–4s', from pre-school into reception class. Love wasn't mentioned, although as can thankfully be seen from the references above, well-being and emotional health featured quite heavily.

Along with all the good ideas for building familiarity and helping children get used to new people and places, was a sense that children needed resilience for change. As the parent of a child adopted from the care system I've learnt a lot about the tremendous capacity that children can have for surviving change – some children have never experienced stability and assume that parents, along with homes and siblings, come and go, changing on a regular (or more likely, irregular) basis. Surely they must be experts at handling day-to-day change and be able to just breeze through transitions – they've done it often enough, haven't they? And yet, these children can struggle dreadfully with the slightest transition – leaving the classroom to go to assembly, finishing an activity before lunch, coming in from the playground, going out to the playground. They struggle to reunite with their carer at the end of the day just as much as they resist leaving them in the morning. I knew that INSECURE ATTACHMENT was at the root of my child's struggle with transition – so perhaps SECURE ATTACHMENT and the emotional resilience that comes as a result of it, might be fundamental to successful transitions?

This book is an attempt to understand transitions from the perspective of attachment theory and what we know about the development of the brain; to utilise the concept of primary and secondary attachment figures in providing consistency and to reposition them in the context of childcare and education.

Three types of transitions

Transitions can be described as horizontal, vertical or internal. Vertical transitions are the major changes that take place as a child moves through the early years system of services towards and including school. Internal transitions occur when a child moves within a setting because of their age or stage e.g. from the 'under 3s' area to the 'over 3s'. Horizontal transitions are much broader and include those that a child experiences:

- on a day-to-day basis, e.g. from home to childminder, then to nursery or playgroup and back home again;
- concurrently during the week, e.g. attending more than one daycare, after school provision, playgroup etc; being cared for by different people on different days, e.g. within the family;
- throughout the day within one setting, e.g. having multiple carers working in shifts or dealing with different aspects of care;
- in the natural course of the day, e.g. moving to a different space for lunch; from one adult-directed activity to another; dealing with unfamiliar people, places or experiences etc.

Each chapter contains some reflection tasks. These link practice to theory and also allow the reader to reflect personally on their own experiences and to assess how they relate to their opinions and judgements, their motivations and training needs as well as current practice.

Chapters 1 and 2 look at attachment theory and the development of the brain and how they link with transition. I have also drawn on the work of Dorothy Y. Selleck and others, who challenge the mute acceptance and 'normalisation' of multiple transitions in the lives of our youngest children. The fact that these transitions take place at a time when children are instinctively resisting separation from the people most important to them (it seems children really do know what's good for them) must surely cause us to question why we continue to let it happen? But mostly we don't question it at all – and a brief walk through the history of early years provision and services for children in Chapter 3 shows that, despite the UK having had some of the foremost thinkers and innovators in early childhood practice, we have still arrived at a place where services are fragmented and families are faced with a 'patchwork' of provision to supposedly 'choose' from.

Chapter 4 encourages us to put ourselves in the 'shoes of the child' by first reflecting on our own experience of change and the strategies that help us, as adults, to deal with transitions. This chapter includes scenarios of children and families experiencing transition, and the ways that practitioners manage and support them (or not) through the process. These scenarios are amalgamations of people and situations I have known and experienced and do not relate directly back to real people.

Chapter 5 looks at some real life examples of strategies that have been used to either remove a transition or reduce the stressful impact of change in some way. This includes a consideration of the key person approach which builds on our understanding of attachment theory and the need for secure secondary attachment figures to provide continuity and stability through attuned, nurturing relationships.

Chapter 6 considers how best to support children's emotional well-being during the inevitable transitions and provides some practical strategies and ideas for use with all children, as well as at different stages. It concludes with an audit that draws together the suggestions and can be used to promote discussion as well as evaluate current policies and processes for transition.

Chapters 1–5 conclude with a summary that hopefully clarifies the main points and leads to implications for practice that suggest action to be taken or maintained.

The Conclusion points to ways forward to integrate policies and practice relating to transition, with what we know and understand about how attachment and relationship build resilience and positive dispositions to embrace change and thrive during challenging times.

Throughout all chapters, I have included reference to children with special needs who are most vulnerable in times of transition. Their experience of change is heightened by their particular circumstances, and by the bias and extra challenge they or their families might experience as a result. I have not created a separate category or chapter for them – attending to their needs is not an add-on to what we do regularly for every other child. My intention rather is to weave a thread through this text that points to the conviction that what is good practice for our most vulnerable children is good practice for all. If our aim is to provide an environment that meets *their* need for continuity, security and stability through secure attachment and relationship then we will be putting it in place for *all* children. Although generalisations can be made, the specifics of flexible, personalised, transition support will be different and particular for each and every child.

A note on terminology

There is ongoing debate about how best to label the various categories within the early years workforce. In the absence, so far, of anything more definitive, I have chosen, for the purposes of this book, to continue with the practice of referring to anyone who is qualified to work with young children, as an early years 'practitioner'. This includes people with teaching qualifications, education and early childhood degrees as well as Early Years Professionals (EYP), Nursery Nurses (NNEB) and staff with recognised NVQs, whether they work in childminding, in childcare and nursery education settings or in schools and other establishments. I believe it is important that our profession continues to include the highest of qualifications and the full spectrum of training and experience. We share a common goal in the quality of our practice and the care with which we attend to the needs of the children and families we work with. Education is a crucial element of our practice and teachers – and the insights that come from a teaching background and initial training – are vital in the early years workforce. What sets early years teachers apart from teachers of other age groups and increases their status within the teaching profession, in my view, is the richness and breadth of experience they gain from working with experienced and differently qualified people focused very particularly on the needs of our youngest children. Where there is an emphasis on the specific nature of childminding I have used the term childminder, but in all other instances, childminders and teachers are embraced in the term 'practitioner' – and I leave it to the reader to recognise what fits with their particular circumstance.

1

Attachment theory and transitions

What is attachment theory and why does it matter?

In this chapter we will look at attachment theory and how it relates to transitions, looking closely at both secure and insecure attachment and some of the factors that influence them. The chapter discusses children's relationships with their attachment figures and how these relate to their well-being, particularly at times of transition.

REFLECTION TASK

Have a think about . . .

What comes to mind when you hear the words **ATTACH** and **ATTACHMENT**? Make a list.

Here are a few suggestions – you're bound to think of more.

connect	fondness for	belonging
tied to	add-ons	computer files
linked	hoovers	

What emotions do these words trigger in you? They might be positive or negative.

Now think about the word **UNATTACHED** and make another list.

unconnected disconnected	untied	free
not known abandoned	separated	

Once again, think about your emotional response.

Hold onto those thoughts. We will come back to them later in the chapter.

What does attachment have to do with transition?

Understanding attachment theory is an important step towards understanding two very important aspects of transition:

■ a secure base
■ emotional resilience.

In her book *From Birth to One: The Year of Opportunity* (2003) Maria Robinson writes:

> Development is all about transitions. All our lives are a series of transitions: conception to birth, birth to toddlerhood, to pre-schooler, school-age child to adolescent, adolescent to adult, adult to our final transition – when we die. Throughout this time we have the capacity for change and adaptation, but we all need a starting point. Our universal starting point is when we emerge from our mothers into the world as a bundle of raw, unregulated emotion. From that first moment through our primary experiences of need and response comes the formation of the first feelings of emotional security and safety.
>
> (Robinson 2003:17–18)

Attachment theory focuses on the development of those first feelings of emotional security – on how and why they need to happen, and what happens if they don't develop as well as they should.

Attachment theory

The theory of attachment was first outlined in 1958. More than half a century later, it continues to be a subject of much research and debate.

The most prominent name in the field of attachment theory has to be that of John Bowlby. His theory was linked to his understanding of the concept of parenting, and he began exploring how a baby's early experience might have an impact on the overall well-being of the adult they will eventually become.

In attachment theory, an attachment is a bond that develops from a child's instinctive need for safety, security and protection. Earlier thinking had been that this instinctive need was driven by the need for food – which the mother provided in the form of breast milk. But Bowlby was struck by the work of Lorenz (1935), who noticed that young ducklings instinctively followed their mother figures everywhere, even though they knew how to feed themselves from a very early stage. This theory of 'imprinting' suggested to Bowlby that there might be another instinctive drive behind the urge of a child to attach themselves to a parent.

In Bowlby's theory, this urge for attachment is about more than just food. It is an instinctive drive for safety, security and protection and a baby's survival depends on it. But there is another dimension to this that has since been borne out by technological advances in neuroscience. Babies are also instinctively triggering the responses and sensory stimulation from others that will help build their brains. To do this effectively, they need to keep these important people close by and to engage with them as often as possible.

Although we might think of babies as helpless and completely dependent on others for their care and protection, babies are also extremely active in making sure we give them all the attention they know they need! Their instinctive attachment-seeking behaviours attract the caregiving behaviours of others. It is as though babies – and the people around them – are programmed to respond to each other. It is more than just the parent *knowing* that a baby needs care – the baby is triggering something within the parent's brain that provides the encouragement or drive to respond and take care of them. Think of a crying baby and just how difficult it can be to ignore! But equally, there are also positive 'feel-good' reactions in the parent's brain that drive the motivation to respond. This is linked to hormones and brain chemicals, such as oxytocin, which, when present, benefit both the baby and the parent.

Regulating emotions

None of us is born with the ability to regulate our own emotions, but babies soon learn that when they signal distress (which will feel uncontrollable and intolerable to them), a responsive caregiver can soothe the distress and 'regulate' the feeling. Being able to rely on this responsive caregiver not only helps soothe the distress, it also builds pathways in the brain through repeated positive experiences, so that the child is able to internalise that sense of security as they begin to work out how to do it for themselves in healthy ways. The distress triggers attachment-seeking behaviours which, if responded to appropriately, reinforce the attachment (see Figure 1).

Sadly, not all caregivers are reliable in their responses. There are a variety of reasons why this might be (see 'Factors that can heighten the risk of poor attachment', p. 8), but the impact is the same. The baby signals distress and doesn't get a response, or the response is one that doesn't make them feel better. Remember, the distress feels uncontrollable and intolerable – and no-one is making it go away. The baby's brain is flooded with cortisol – a stress hormone. A young baby who feels bad has only one way of getting attention, and that is to cry – long and loud, probably. This might be enough to force an adult to meet their needs now, at least in part. But for an adult who isn't well enough regulated themselves, this might reinforce their negative feelings and make it even less likely that they can provide the love and soothing attention the baby is crying out for, as well as any physical need they may also have.

If the responses are erratic – sometimes the baby gets what they need, sometimes they don't – the child learns that their important adults can't be relied on and they have to live with a high level of uncertainty. This doesn't feel good, nor does it

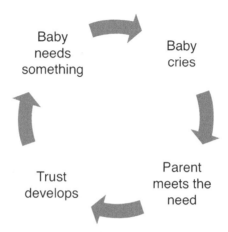

FIGURE 1 The regulation cycle (adapted from S. Gott (2009) *Teach to Inspire Better Behaviour: Strategies for coping with aggressive, disruptive and unpredictable behaviours.* London: Optimus Education).

help the child to learn positive patterns of self-regulation. Worse still, if the child very rarely, if ever, gets the responses they need, their only option is to find ways to self-regulate or soothe themselves, and these are unlikely to be healthy.

Richard Bowlby (son of John Bowlby) has carried on his father's work on attachment. In his paper *The Need for Secondary Attachment Figures in Daycare (2007)* he describes how the natural attachment-seeking behaviours can be deactivated when a baby's primary attachment figure is not available to them.

> There is a wide range of instinctive and learned dissociative behaviours that babies and toddlers adopt when they are unable to reach an attachment figure: some appear unaffected by the experience of separation, and others may be over boisterous or aggressive, some continue to be active but are rather subdued or withdrawn, and some quietly occupy themselves alone and appear to be undemanding and 'easy children', whilst others may be overly compliant or obedient and unusually co-operative. At the extreme end of the dissociative spectrum is the 'freeze and surrender' response of blanking or stilling. Babies' instinct to de-activate their attachment seeking response under stress in the absence of an attachment figure probably originated as an emergency measure to reduce the risk of being detected in the natural environment of evolution.
>
> (R. Bowlby 2007)

Assessing the quality of attachment

Psychologist Mary Ainsworth developed a research technique to assess the quality of attachment in 12- to 18-month-old children. It is known as the 'Strange Situation Test', and it allowed researchers to observe the reactions and patterns of behaviour when children of this age were left in an unfamiliar place with an adult who was equally unfamiliar to them (Ainsworth et al. 1978). The way the child responded to being separated and then reunited with their parent was seen as an indicator of the security of the attachment. Because a securely attached child has built up a memory of the parent as someone who keeps them safe, at this age they will likely cry when the parent leaves and generally be happy and enthusiastic about seeing them when they come back. An insecurely attached child might react in a variety of different ways.

This research provided a very important starting point for understanding the difference between secure and insecure attachment. It is also very relevant when we are thinking about the transitions babies and young children very often experience, and a challenge to the assumption that 'not crying' is a good sign. We will look at this again in Chapter 6 when we think about practical strategies for supporting the daily handover rituals from parent to carer.

What does secure attachment look like?

A securely attached child is building up an image of themselves as someone who is lovable and well-loved. As Maria Robinson says, 'the child who is loved, encouraged, respected and comforted is able to learn about the world in a context of emotional safety, and about themselves as fundamentally loveable' (Robinson 2003:41). This is because of the responses they get from the adults and others around them. They have built up a memory of their parent(s) as someone who makes them feel safe. They know that when something happens that makes them feel insecure, or scared, or uncomfortable, these reliable people come and take care of it and, soon enough, they will feel fine again. Because of this, they can cope when things aren't exactly as they want them to be and although they may well get upset, angry, sad or anxious, they trust others to help them and don't stay agitated for too long. They are building that all-important 'emotional resilience' that is essential for good mental health.

These important feelings of security mean that they feel safe enough to take risks and to 'branch out' and experiment and explore the world around them, knowing that someone else is looking out for them. Their significant relationships are based on love and affection, sensitivity, attunement and reciprocity. These relationships provide a 'secure base' and help to build their confidence and self-esteem. It is thought that a majority of children have attachments that are reasonably secure, because the majority of parents are able (or are supported well enough) to behave in ways that provide their children with these secure feelings. They know they are 'held in mind' by their important people and increasingly, as they get older, this helps them feel secure even when they can't see them.

We will come back to this important consideration of being 'held in mind', because it has a crucial role to play in the way we cope with separation and change.

Disrupt and repair

Just as importantly, children with secure attachments also learn that a 'good enough' attachment isn't damaged just because they've done something naughty or their parent is in a bad mood. The 'disruption and repair' cycle (Schore 1994) is a vital part of attachment. A child needs to know that a disagreement isn't the end of the world and is reassured by the good feelings that come when their important adults tune in with them again and relationship is restored. This fundamental feature of secure attachment is linked to the idea of a safe or secure base that is unconditional in its security.

This is a key feature of Bowlby's attachment theory and plays a big part in enabling a child to grow into adulthood feeling emotionally secure and self-confident. It seems to me to have a crucial link with transitions too, as this predictability and reassurance – this sense of unconditional love and regard – helps to reinforce a positive sense of self. It helps maintain our emotional stability during times of change.

What does insecure attachment look like?

Insecure attachment is complicated, and the 'Strange Situation' research identified three different categories of insecure attachment. Bowlby (1988:140–141) described them as:

- anxious avoidant
- anxious resistant
- disorganised–disoriented.

Anxious avoidant attachment is considered the most common of the three categories. In the 'Strange Situation Test' the child seems not to mind that the parent has left, is easily distracted by toys and shows little or no response when the parent returns. We think this is because the child has already learnt (from the signals and behaviour of the parent) that it is not a good thing to show your emotions, whatever they might be. This could be anger, sadness or even fear.

Although this lack of emotion is often thought of as a cultural approach (for example, the British 'stiff upper lip'), it is very likely that it is repeated down the generations because parents themselves have never learnt to manage their own emotions. This makes it hard for them to tolerate negative states such as distress, fear and anger in their own children.

The parent can't help the child regulate or think about their feelings, so the child just learns to hide or suppress them because they don't want to upset or anger the parent. As Sue Gerhardt describes in *Why Love Matters: How affection shapes a baby's brain*, these children 'learn to appear calm and unconcerned, but when measured, their heart rate and autonomic arousal is rocketing' (Gerhardt 2004:26).

This is potentially very significant when we think about children coping with change, who appear, on the surface, to be dealing well with separation.

Anxious resistant attachment is also sometimes referred to as ambivalent attachment. In the Strange Situation the child shows distress when the parent leaves, but connects easily with the unfamiliar adult. When the parent returns the child might be either ambivalent or angry with them.

This child has learnt not to be sure of the parent's attention; they can't predict whether they will be comforting or not. The child's coping strategy is to be permanently on guard. They feel they must be constantly demanding attention, either anxiously or angrily. This is because they don't feel 'held in mind' and are fearful that they might be forgotten or abandoned. They will also attach themselves 'ambivalently' to any available adult in an attempt to reduce their intolerable feelings and keep themselves safe. They live with high levels of unpredictability which is stressful and can generate high levels of cortisol (see the section on 'Brain chemistry: Stress hormones' in Chapter 2). This can affect not just their emotional well-being but also their physical health and ability to learn (Gerhardt 2004:78–79). Once again, this has potential significance when we think about our expectations of children continuing to learn while they are coping with change.

The most severe of the three categories is 'disorganised' or disoriented attachment. The term 'disorganised' is used in its clinical sense and so it's probably best to think of it as describing the erratic and seemingly random reactions displayed by a child who has developed no regular strategies for coping with stress. Hardly any of their experiences of being parented will have been good enough. This is likely to have happened where the parents have been overwhelmed by some trauma that has not been processed properly, such as severe loss, neglect or abuse, and the likelihood is that they themselves are attachment disordered. These children are generally considered to be 'at risk' and may well end up in the care system, where frequent changes of placement can make attachment even more difficult. They are going to find any kind of change threatening and will need very careful support through the regular transitions of everyday life and education.

What these different categories have in common is the lack of a 'secure base'. Although these children may have experienced degrees of physical care and affection it is always either erratic or conditional, e.g. 'mummy won't love you if you behave like that'. There is no certainty for these children that their parents themselves are strong and robust enough for the challenges of parenthood and able to be there for them, no matter what.

'Internal working model'

Bowlby believed that the quality of our attachment relationships helps to build 'an internal working model' for each of us, that describes the way in which we view the world. Maria Robinson suggests that 'our internal working model guides the way in which we feel about ourselves and how we approach or withdraw to new people and situations' (Robinson 2011:55). The internal working model of a child who has not had 'good enough' early attachment experiences is going to be different to that of a child whose experience has been mostly good. The former child's approach to change and transition is not going to be based on the expectation that their needs will be met in this new situation.

Dr Patricia Crittenden, a developmental psychopathologist who worked with Ainsworth, holds the view that it is self-preservation and the need for protection from danger that drive our attachment behaviours, and that attachment classifications are fluid in that they change and adapt over time and in different circumstances (Crittenden and Claussen 2000). This could mean that a range of behaviours might accompany feelings of anxiety and emotional uncertainty in unfamiliar situations. Robinson believes that this 'can sound a warning note to those who try to classify a child's behaviour in absolute terms of their potential secure or insecure attachment' (Robinson 2011:66).

It is important for us as practitioners to remember this. It is not our role to make judgements about the quality of attachment between a child and their parents because we are not clinically trained to do so. It is, however, our responsibility to be open to understanding more about attachment in order to better understand the behaviours and needs of the children and parents we work with, as well as the importance of our own role in building attachment and relationships with them.

Factors that can heighten the risk of poor attachment

We need to be mindful of the things that get in the way of children's secure attachments. First of all, we have to consider the changes that have taken place in western culture and society in recent times. Fewer of us now experience life in extended families where opportunities to rehearse and practise childrearing are plentiful. This may mean that parents today (and young parents in particular) don't get the same chances to absorb all the essential elements of responsiveness and 'tuning in' to the needs of babies that support strong attachments. For some, their own needs may not have been well enough met to allow them to be ready or able to disconnect the baby's needs from their own, and to be emotionally available to them.

There is a long list of other possible reasons why a parent might find it hard to be physically and emotionally available to their baby in the vital early months. This could be as a result of:

- pre-natal stress or birth trauma, e.g. relating to the mother's circumstances, premature birth or medical interventions;
- extended or repeated separations, e.g. if the mother or baby is in hospital;
- mother's post-natal depression;
- child's undiagnosed or unresolved painful illness, e.g. colic, ear infections;
- multiple changes in caregiver, e.g. foster placements;
- parental history of drug/substance abuse;

- family bereavement;
- parents or carers with their own insecure or disordered attachments and other mental health issues (adapted from Bombèr, 2007:21).

It is important to remember that many of these circumstances will have been beyond the parent's control. Bowlby and subsequent researchers have been very clear about this.

> In thus underlining the very great influence that a child's mother has on his development, it is necessary also to consider what has led a mother to adopt the style of mothering she does. One major influence on this is the amount of emotional support, or lack of it, she herself is receiving at the time. Another is the form of mothering that she herself received when a child. Once these factors are recognised, as they have been by many analytically oriented clinicians long since, the idea of blaming parents evaporates and is replaced by a therapeutic approach.
>
> (Bowlby 1988:142)

Sadly, the tendency to want to blame parents remains strong in society at large, but we have to recognise that blame and criticism don't help to change someone's attitude or method of parenting, nor can they break a generational cycle of emotional neglect.

It is also true that poverty and deprivation don't automatically lead to poor attachment – far from it, in fact. But we must never underestimate the impact of difficult circumstances on the physical and mental health of parents and the direct impact that this can have on their capacity to be responsive to their children. Emotionally vulnerable adults trying to parent in difficult circumstances have the odds stacked against them. As we face the likelihood of financially unstable times, it becomes even more important that we work to build future generations of emotionally secure and stable young people able to withstand global economic and environmental insecurity.

Relationships and attachment figures

Richard Bowlby describes the special nature of the relationship with attachment figures.

> In attachment theory, the term *primary* attachment figure refers to the person with whom a child develops their main lifelong emotional bond, and whom they most want to be comforted by when they are frightened or hurt – usually but not necessarily their birth mother. The term *secondary* attachment figure refers to the few special people in a child's life with whom they have developed a close subsidiary or secondary attachment bond, such as siblings, grandparents,

nannies, childminders and especially fathers who have their own unique bond. Having three or more such people will usually increase children's resilience and act as a protective factor throughout childhood. These are the people who can provide babies and toddlers with comfort and security in the absence of a primary attachment figure, and act as a secure base and haven of safety.

(R. Bowlby 2007)

These special relationships are affectionate and sensitive to a child's needs. They provide the child with enough attuned and predictable responses to reassure them that 'if push came to shove' their carers could put aside their own needs in order to meet those of the child. This doesn't mean constantly jumping to the child's demands. It is more about a relaxed, affectionate response that is tailor-made to suit the particular needs and states of the child at any given time. 'Tuning in' to a baby's changing mood or motivations is important not just in ensuring the right kind of response. It also helps a baby to learn about themselves – to develop a strong sense of 'self' and an appreciation of who they are and what it means to be 'them'.

In strong, extended families, there is usually enough 'back up' in the form of secondary attachment figures to provide support and nurture for the parent and also for the child, when the parent is unable to provide what they might need. The job of parenting is hugely demanding – and secondary attachments provide the essential 'safety net' needed in even the most assured and experienced families.

Again, many inexperienced parents nowadays find themselves alone without that strong network of support. Recent developments in early years policy have seen an increase in targeted support for vulnerable families through the work of Sure Start and the development of Children's Centres. It remains to be seen whether subsequent governments will continue to appreciate the importance of knowledgeable support and outreach for all families – or whether a deficit view of poor parenting among the disadvantaged will lead to an increase in targeted parental 'instruction' courses. Either way, inexperienced parents need to be supported by strong networks of knowledgeable others, professional or otherwise, and having 'key people' in early years settings is an important element of this. We shall look more closely at the key person approach in Chapter 5.

Held in mind

Just thinking about feeling unattached to anything or anybody – to not be known or even thought about by others – can be distressing. So let's reassure ourselves with thoughts of the people to whom we are close, whom we care about and who care about us, even if they are not actually close by at this precise moment.

To begin with, a baby *needs* to know their attachment figures are close by in order to feel safe. In an evolutionary sense, the baby knows their only chance for survival is if there is always someone around to protect them from predators.

REFLECTION TASK

Have another think about . . .

The thoughts and emotional responses you had to the first 'Let's think about . . .' task.

Now imagine you are floating in space – attached by a life-line to a spaceship. How important is that 'attachment'?

- Why?
- How do you feel about it?
- What does it provide you with?
  - Security? Air to breathe?
  - Connection to others? To home, safety, survival?

And now imagine how it would feel if that life-line were to be cut and you were left floating in space, unconnected to anything.

- What's your immediate emotional response?
  - A sense of freedom?
  - Fear and panic?

What is going to happen to you if you are not connected in any way with any other thing in the universe – **if you are not known**?

Now try and imagine an earthly version of that.

For a few months (nine, if you were lucky) you were connected by a life-line (umbilical cord) to another human being. That line was cut when you were born, but what if you were never again connected or attached enough to any other person to feel that same degree of connection? Would you feel safe enough to take the risk of going out into the unknown – to leave your spaceship without an airline?

- Would you survive?
- Would you even be able to breathe?

If the care is continuous and reliably predictable, then the feeling of being safe gradually grows and stays with the child even if they are on their own for a short while in another room. A child who is securely attached is able to carry with them that feeling of being nurtured and cared for – and cared about. They have that special sense that they are 'held in mind' by their parents and wider family.

Jeree Pawl has written a very illuminating article about this important process. Dr Pawl describes how '[t]he powerful wish to know and be known becomes more possible.'

sometime around seven to nine months, something new is happening. The baby's mother points at something and, instead of staring fixedly at her mother's hand, the baby looks where her mother is pointing. Soon the baby – who frequently has stretched out her hand towards something that is out of reach, grunting as she strains – points instead. She turns to look to see if her mother gets the idea. She does. The baby has made the discovery that her mother has a mind! The child can now have the intention to affect someone's mind and to be a reader of minds. The baby now knows her wishes and intentions can be in someone else's mind. The powerful wish to know and be known becomes more possible. This is a complex achievement that emerged from the child's experiences. All along this child has felt noticed, responded to, and has been aware of her impact in the moment and over time.

(Pawl 2006:2)

Once we have understood this concept, it is easy to see how crucial it is to our sense of well-being at times of transition. We need to feel 'cared about' as well as 'cared for'. Moving from a place or situation in which we feel 'known' into one in which we feel 'unknown' raises our insecurity about having our needs met. This feeling of security in being 'known' and ultimately not being all alone in the world is perhaps at the heart of all human emotion. It's something we are likely to take for granted – when it's securely in place. But some children, sadly, do not have any certainty that they are held in mind by the people that matter to them, and for them the world is a very scary and stressful place – there is no lifeline to help them with survival (O'Connor 2007/2008).

But even the most securely attached child will need help with all of this at transition times. A vitally important part of our job as practitioners helping children settle into an early years setting or school is keeping the parents in mind for the child, as well as reassuring them that they themselves also exist for their parents, when they are apart from them. We will look at practical ways of doing this in Chapter 6.

A secure base and emotional resilience

Let's look again at these two important aspects of transition highlighted at the beginning of the chapter.

Bowlby's work has helped us to see that having the certainty of a 'secure base' where we are known and 'held in mind' is fundamental to our mental health. It must also be fundamental to our approach to transitions as we seek to provide a secure base for our children so that they can safely take the risk of moving away from us – as parents, childminders, practitioners – and onto the next stage in their lives.

Contrary to what we might expect, we don't build healthy emotional resilience by surviving lots of negative experiences. It's the positive experiences of being warmly loved and cared for, responded to and valued unconditionally that build emotional resilience in our brains. Positive, loving responses help us build an image of ourselves as lovable and capable and teach us to be able to regulate ourselves in times of crisis. As we will explore further in Chapter 4, the more negative experiences we have, the less resilience we seem to have for negative experiences in the future. We might develop survival strategies, but they probably won't be healthy ones.

This is linked to the chemistry of our brains and the way our bodies respond to events and circumstances that our brains perceive as threats. To make sense of this we need to know a certain amount about the way our brains develop, and we will look more closely at this in Chapter 2.

Health warning

Reading and thinking about attachment is likely to make us all reflect on our own attachments and early childhood experiences. This is good because it helps us to understand and empathise with the children and families we work with. It can also be distressing, however, as we uncover aspects of our own lives that have impacted on our emotional well-being. Understanding attachment can help us understand ourselves very much better – but please make sure you seek help and advice if exploring this subject causes you distress or makes you feel unsafe.

Summary

This chapter aimed to provide just a brief exploration of some of the most important aspects of attachment theory.

- Early attachment experiences are important for brain development and can have a lifelong impact on how we deal with change and uncertainty.

- Babies and young children instinctively resist separation in order to keep themselves safe.

- 'Good enough' attachment experiences build feelings of security and well-being and increase our emotional resilience.

- Poor attachment experiences cause stress which can be displayed in different ways.

- We all benefit from strong secondary attachments that support our primary attachments.

- Strong secondary attachments can possibly compensate for insecure primary attachments.

Implications for our practice

With an increased understanding of attachment theory, we are better equipped to:

■ recognise the importance of strong primary and secondary attachments and the risks that insecure attachment poses for lifelong well-being;

■ be open to adapting our approaches as knowledge and understanding of attachment theory increasingly unfold;

■ ensure that our interactions with children are warm, responsive and 'tuned in' to them as individuals;

■ support families where secure attachments may be at risk and work with them to create strong secondary attachments in the setting for the child;

■ use our knowledge and understanding of attachment theory to develop our approach to supporting transitions;

■ recognise our own attachment patterns and issues and be aware of how they may impact on our relationships with children and on our childcare practices.

2

Brain development and the impact of transitions

This chapter provides some basic information on what is currently known and understood about brain development and how this links with theories of attachment and emotional resilience. The chapter also explores the nature of stress hormones and brain chemicals and why these are important when we are thinking about transition.

Attachment theory and the brain

Since Bowlby's day, there has been a huge increase in the technology that allows us to know more about brain development, although much of what we are finding out now through neuroscience seems to confirm Bowlby's theories of attachment.

Although we tend to think of neuroscience as a very complex and difficult subject, acquiring some basic information about the way our brains function is a really useful tool in helping our understanding of the emotions we associate with change and transitions, as well as helping us to understand behaviour in general.

In her book *The Science of Parenting*, Margot Sunderland makes the point that we don't have just one brain – we have three, the reptilian, the mammalian and the rational brain. This is based on the belief that our brains have evolved with the human race and each region of the brain represents another layer of development in evolutionary terms. Sue Jennings, in her book *Healthy Attachments and Neuro-Dramatic Play*, comments that not all neuroscientists now believe in the 'triune' (Maclean 1990) or 'layered brain' theory, but that it continues to be a useful way of helping us understand brain function (Figure 2). She quotes L. Cozolino (2006), who wrote, 'Think of it as a brain within a brain within a brain, each successive layer devoting itself to increasingly complex functions and abilities' (Jennings 2011:34).

Reptilian brain: instincts

We'll start with the reptilian brain – the oldest and deepest part of our brains. It is described like this because it functions in the same way in all vertebrate creatures.

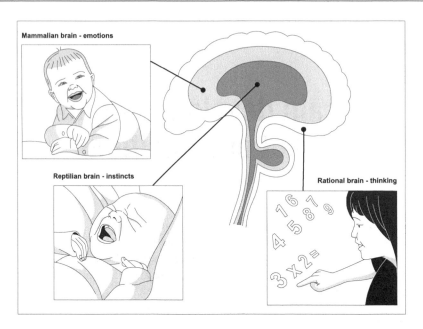

FIGURE 2 The three-fold nature of the human brain (adapted from Julio Rocha do Amaral & Jorge Martins de Oliveira, *The Three Units of the Human Brain*; available at www.cerebromente.org.br/n05/mente/limbic_i.htm (accessed 29 May 2012)).

The reptilian brain is all about survival. It activates the instinctive behaviour and bodily functions that we need to stay alive. These include:

- breathing
- temperature
- movement
- hunger
- digestion and elimination.

This part of the brain is also responsible for another set of instinctive survival behaviours commonly referred to as 'fight, flight or freeze'. We will return to look at these more closely as they have important implications for the way we cope with perceived threat, including change of any kind.

Mammalian brain: emotions

The next region of our brain to evolve was the mammalian brain. Its structure and systems are almost exactly the same as those found in all mammals. This is sometimes referred to as the 'emotional' brain, the 'lower' brain, or the limbic system. Strong emotions are activated in the mammalian brain and it also acts as an early warning system, helping to control those primitive responses of fight, flight or freeze.

Margot Sunderland (2006:19) describes how it is responsible for activating

■ fear
■ rage
■ distress

but also for triggering the urge

■ to care and nurture
■ to explore
■ to be playful
■ to bond socially.

The amygdala is located within the mammalian brain and detects potential threat. Understanding how we perceive threat – and the way we react – is very useful when we are thinking about transitions.

Rational brain: thinking

The final part, and the most recent in evolutionary terms, is the rational brain. This is thought of as the 'higher' brain and sometimes referred to as the 'frontal lobes' or the neo-cortex. As the last to evolve, it envelops and surrounds the two older parts of our brain. The reptilian brain sits deeply at the core of our brains, with the mammalian brain between it and the rational brain. This is important when we think of the role our emotional brain has in helping to control our instinctive 'reptilian' survival responses and to inform the higher order 'rational' thinking of our frontal lobes.

Our rational brain has many functions, including:

■ reasoning
■ reflection
■ problem solving
■ creativity and imagination
■ self-awareness
■ empathy (Sunderland 2006:18).

It is this part of our brains that has led to great human achievements, but, as Sunderland (2006:18) points out, 'when cut off from the mammalian brain's social emotion systems, it is also responsible for appalling cruelties'. The point of this statement is to remind us that in order to function well, we need all the parts of our brain to be co-ordinating with each other. If one part is activated more strongly than the others and becomes dominant, then it has a powerful impact on our perceptions and the way we conduct our lives.

This co-ordination depends on the different parts of the brain being able to 'speak' to each other, and they do this through the neural pathways that build as a result of the experiences a child has. Each sensory experience fires a connection between the cells in our brains. Repeated experiences strengthen these connections or pathways, allowing the brain to take shortcuts each time the experience happens again. It is important to remember that in the early years of a child's life, the higher rational brain is still very undeveloped and it is the lower brain that is 'in the driving seat' (Sunderland 2006:22). This means that the primitive impulses and alarm systems of the lower brain will be constantly triggered – and quickly become overwhelming – because the higher brain isn't developed enough yet to help them use reason and rational thought to soothe these powerful emotions and feelings of threat.

Understanding threat

Knowing about the alarm systems lodged deep in the lower brain is very helpful for us as practitioners. We need to understand the emotions and feelings of babies and young children experiencing something they perceive as a threat to their survival. These alarm systems of fear, rage and separation distress are rooted in early human existence. It is believed they are there from birth, in order to keep the baby safe from predators – and ensuring that a parent stays close by is essential to this. Being eaten by a wild animal isn't quite so much of a risk these days, but the constant close protection of a parent is still essential for a twenty-first-century baby who is powerless to protect itself. The infant brain is instinctively programmed to make sure that a parent stays nearby. It triggers the baby to cry loudly if anything startles or alarms them – and particularly if they feel they might have been left alone. Let's not forget, a baby doesn't *know* that a parent who is gone for a short while is ever going to come back.

The alarm systems can kick in at the slightest thing – the brain is fundamentally reacting to the perceived threat and isn't able to rationalise whether the threat is real. Think of the things that might cause a reaction in a baby – a loud noise, a cold draught, a pin prick, a splash of water? The amygdala detects these as THREAT and triggers an immediate distress response from the baby – usually crying. Waking up and sensing no-one around, a baby is likely to cry. Being picked up can help to soothe this distress, but if we keep in mind this notion of 'predators', it becomes easier to see why being picked up, in itself, may not be enough to regulate the baby's emotions. The baby needs to know that they are being held by someone that will keep them safe. After all, they might have been picked up by something that is going to eat them! It is the warm, affectionate, loving responses from a recognised attachment figure that soothe the overwhelming fear of abandonment or threat.

Separation as a threat to survival

The separation distress system in a young child is hypersensitive – it has to stay constantly on the alert for the threat of abandonment. Over time, the repetition of loving and predictable responses will build strong connections in the brain, which will develop the frontal lobes and allow inhibition of this system, so that it becomes not quite so sensitive. As adults we can recognise the feelings and emotions that separation can bring, but we are able to be more rational in understanding that, in general, our survival is not *actually* threatened, even though we may still experience strong emotions related to our fear of abandonment. This early instinctive separation anxiety, however, can last until a child is well over five years old (Sunderland 2006). This is exactly the time period we are concerned with as early years practitioners trying to understand the impact of transitions. The transition from home to care or education outside the home, whether it is to a childminder, daycare provider, play group, nursery or reception class, takes place *when the child's brain is still instinctively programmed to resist that separation.*

Knowing this forces us into the realisation that, in an ideal world, we wouldn't want babies and young children to experience the pain of separation, at least not until their rational brains were well enough developed for them to understand that their survival was not threatened by it. But we don't live in an ideal world. There are many legitimate reasons why a child might have to experience early temporary

separations, and that is exactly why Bowlby stresses the importance of secondary attachment figures. The one thing that most effectively soothes the distress of separation from the primary attachment figure is the responsive presence and affectionate, caring attentions of another familiar carer. This is what happens within families and it can happen outside of the home too, where the affectionate, unconditional response might equally come from the childminder, the key person at daycare, playgroup or nursery or the reception class teacher or teaching assistant. The role of the secondary attachment figure is very important in our understanding of early transitions and we will return to it in later chapters.

Brain chemistry: stress hormones

Margot Sunderland reminds us that it is not over-dramatic to talk of the 'pain' of separation. She writes that 'When a child is suffering because of the absence of a parent, the same parts of the brain are activated as when she is feeling physical pain' (Sunderland 2006:52, citing Ladd et al. 1996 and Sanchez et al. 2001).

Sunderland points out that as a society we are perhaps more ready to recognise and comfort a child's physical pain than we do the emotional pain of separation. We also have a tendency to underestimate the impact of stress on a child's brain – and, ultimately, on their physical and emotional well-being.

Our stress response system enables our bodies to prepare for potential threat. Hormones play an important part in this. Cortisol is a stress hormone that is released by the adrenal glands; its role in the short term is to boost the amount of glucose in the blood. When a baby is distressed and crying, cortisol washes through the body and the brain. If the child is soothed and comforted, then the level of cortisol goes back down. Over time, the same 'normal' experiences (hunger, discomfort, etc.) don't stress the baby out in the same way (i.e. raise their cortisol levels) because they are learning that someone will predictably sort it out for them (Balbernie 2007:1). But if they don't receive the help and comfort they need, then the levels of cortisol remain high. If this happens over a prolonged period, the levels of cortisol become toxic and can damage important parts of the child's developing brain. Because cortisol is a slow-acting chemical, it can take a long time to reduce and so can stay at high levels in the brain for hours. In babies and young children who are constantly exposed to high levels of stress, their systems can become permanently oversensitive and continue to pump out cortisol, although in some high-risk children the levels remain low due to the adaptation that can happen in response to chronic or persistent stress (Balbernie 2007:2). This isn't good either, as low cortisol levels have been linked with a range of emotional and physical issues (Gerhardt 2004:82).

Either way, inappropriate levels of cortisol can have long-term implications for a child's physical, intellectual and emotional well-being in later life. Depression, anxiety disorders, alcohol and substance abuse, and eating and digestive disorders have all been linked with unrelieved stress in early life. Gerhardt describes how being able to switch off the production of cortisol at the right moment seems to be what's important, so that we don't suppress it or become flooded with it. The ability to do this effectively is linked to the security of the attachment process, and the intensity and timing of challenges in our early lives seem to affect the different ways we handle and regulate our emotions (Gerhardt 2004:83–84). Linking this to a child's experience of stressful separation reminds us that some children will react and show us their distress, while others may 'shut down' and appear to be coping, or at least not cause a fuss.

Research also suggests that early stress can have a damaging impact on the structure of the brain by causing cell death in the hippocampus. This part of the lower mammalian brain is important for memory. Adults with a shrunken hippocampus score lower on tests for working memory and verbal reasoning, and it seems that brain scans of very stressed children show their hippocampus to resemble that of an aged person (Sunderland 2006). Because of this, stress in early life is regarded as a risk factor for accelerated aging of the hippocampus. Having a poor working memory affects a child's ability to hold more than one thought in their head at a time, which is an essential skill in mathematics, as well as many other areas of learning.

Research summary

The Science of Parenting (Sunderland 2006) provides a wealth of research information showing the links between cortisol levels in early life and subsequent physical and mental health. This research includes the following:

- Heim, C, Owens, M. J., Plotsky, P. M. and Nemeroff, C. B. (1997) Persistent changes in corticotrophin-releasing factor systems due to early life stress: Relationship to the pathophysiology of major depression and post-traumatic stress disorder. *Psychopharmacology Bulletin, 33,* 185–192.

- Beatson J. and Taryon, S. (2003) Predispositions to depression: the role of attachment. *Australian and New Zealand Journal of Psychiatry,* Apr., 219–225.

- Plotsky P. M., Owens, M. J. and Nemeroff, C. B. (1998) Psychoneuro-endocrinology of depression: Hypothalamic–pituitary–adrenal axis. *Psychiatric Clinics of North America, 21,* 293–307.

- Stam, R., Akkermans, L. M and Wiegant, V. M. (1997) Trauma and the gut: Interactions between stressful experience and intestinal function. *Gut, 40,* 704–709.

- Alfvén, G. (2004) Plasma oxytocin in children with recurrent abdominal pain, *Journal of Pediatric Gastroenterology and Nutrition, 38,* 513–517.

- Jarrett, M. E., Burr, R. L, Cain, K. C., Hertig, V., Weisman, P. and Heitkemper, M. M. (2003) Anxiety and depression are related to autonomic nervous system function in women with irritable bowel syndrome. *Digestive Diseases and Sciences, 48,* 386–394.

- Heaton, K. (1999) *Your bowels*. London: British Medical Association/Dorling Kindersley (p. 34).

- McEwen, B. S. (1999) Stress and the aging hippocampus, *Frontiers in Neuro-endocrinology*, *20*, 49–70.

- Bremner, J. D. and Narayan, M. (1998) The effects of stress on memory and the hippocampus throughout the life cycle: Implications for childhood development and aging. *Developmental Psychology*, *10*, 871–885.

Stress tolerance

There is something of a vicious circle in all of this. Too many changes and separations cause stress, and too much stress makes it difficult to cope with change when it happens. Our 'window' of stress tolerance becomes minimal when an overload of change and inconsistency registers in our brains and bodies as constant or repeated threats. It raises our levels of cortisol and can damage the structures in our brain. Any new change will register quickly as yet more threat and our window of tolerance slams shut, leaving us with no resources with which to handle it.

In his paper *Cortisol and the Early Years*, Robin Balbernie (2007) describes how, 'Over the first year of life children generally learn to dampen their cortisol response to experiences of stress, and this ability is linked to the quality of the caregiving they have received.' He quotes research that suggests 'infants in secure attachment relationships are less likely to elevate cortisol, even if they are distressed, whereas infants in insecure relationships do' (Gunnar and Cheatham, 2003:204). He goes on to raise questions about the impact of cortisol on young children experiencing poor-quality daycare and the likelihood that vulnerable children with already poor attachments will be worst affected. He then links this to research demonstrating that 'children who produce higher levels of cortisol during normal days at nursery school have a harder time sustaining attention than do children with lower cortisol levels' (Gunner and Barr, 1998:5) and that a 'flood of stress hormones can produce toxic effects on the development of brain systems responsible for self-regulation' (Siegal, 1999:295).

More recent studies in Germany with toddlers showed similar results with regard to day nurseries (Ahnert, Gunnar, Lamb and Barthel, 2004). Three months after the settling-in period, cortisol levels among the children continued to indicate chronic mild stress even among children judged to have secure attachments. In her summary of the research (published on the What About the Children? web-site), Dr Claire Sansom notes that it is 'clear that day nurseries are stressful places for one year olds and that even secure attachment to their main caregivers does not buffer them from this stress'.

Brain chemistry: feel-good chemicals

But it's not all bad news. Our bodies also have the capacity to produce hormones and brain chemicals that make us feel good. Some of these are present immediately after birth when bonding and attachment first begin. Opioids are brain chemicals that help relieve pain and contribute to our general sense of well-being. Oxytocin is an anti-stress chemical that is vital to our feelings of safety and comfort. It can also inhibit our stress response system and reduce the amount of cortisol released. Margot Sunderland describes the powerful effect of these chemicals in combination: 'these neurochemicals can bring us the deepest sense of calm and contentment, with the capacity to take life's stresses in stride' (Sunderland 2006: 86). Sounds like exactly what we need when facing the stress of change and transition!

So how do we make sure children have enough of these important anti-stress chemicals? Well, the simple answer is that they are activated in the brain every time a child experiences warm, caring connections with others. Hugs and cuddles, affectionate strokes and massage, the warmth of another body snuggled next to you, all stimulate the release of opioids and oxytocin – not just for the child but also in the connected adult. This two-way process is important as it reminds us that children are very susceptible to our moods and body language. Close, physical contact with a calm adult can help soothe an agitated child, because it stimulates the flow of opioids. Equally, a tense, anxious adult attempting to calm a distressed child is likely to have the opposite effect and increase cortisol flow.

Concerns about physical safety and child protection issues have tended to cloud people's judgement about close physical contact with young children. It is undeniable that safeguards need to exist, but we must also uphold what we as practitioners know – that we cannot do our job well if we are not able to hold and comfort, snuggle and stroke, hug and tickle and generally enfold our children in warm embraces of care and affection. And here we have the scientific rationale for why our children need it and why we need to keep on doing it!

REFLECTION TASK

Have a think about ... three children you have observed struggle with transition.

- What alerted you to the fact that the child was struggling with transition?
- What behaviours did you see?
- Were they broadly the same, or different in each child?

Understanding fight, flight or freeze

When the brain perceives a threat, it triggers reactions in the body to deal with it. As Sunderland describes it, the body is 'primed for action' as, among other things, the heart rate increases, the muscles tense and the appetite is suppressed (Sunderland 2006:44). This is all to prepare us to 'fight, flight or freeze' – the three actions for which we are instinctively primed in times of physical threat. The most significant regular threat that our evolutionary ancestors had to face was being attacked by something bigger or stronger than themselves. In that instance, the body would need to be prepared to challenge the attacker (fight), to run away from it (flight) or to stand still in the hope it wouldn't see or be threatened by them (freeze). These reactions are still there in our own responses to threat in our everyday lives. This is sometimes because of healthy responses to actual threat. But sometimes they are our instinctive responses to a *perceived* threat that have become habitual through experience.

This is relevant to our understanding of children experiencing transition. For some children, repeated negative experiences of transition can result in strong feelings of threat and anxiety. They might:

- fight – with prolonged crying and resistance, aggressive or challenging behaviour;
- take flight – by running from the situation, either literally in the sense that they try to run home, or emotionally by resisting attention from unfamiliar people; or
- freeze, by being physically withdrawn, staying in the same place, not moving or moving very slowly, as well as shutting down emotionally.

As practitioners we might see these kinds of behaviours quite frequently, but how often do we trace them back to the child's response to the 'threat' of being away from home?

Neuroscience provides us with evidence that not only our bodies, but also our brains prepare for fight, flight or freeze, by activating the parts of the brain most needed for the impulse to protect ourselves and temporarily shutting down everything else. If a car is about to run you over you're not likely at that moment to be interested in what make it is or the colour of its bodywork. In the same way, a child experiencing the kinds of hyper-arousal described above isn't likely to be interested in the story being read to them, or curious about the maths problem in front of them.

Uncertainty as threat

The amygdala is the part of the brain thought to be responsible for threat detection; more recent research (Herry et al. 2007) seems to suggest that it is also activated by uncertainty, which can provoke just as big a stress reaction in some people as

REFLECTION TASK

Have a think about . . . behaviours you have observed in your setting. Have you observed children who:

- became aggressive and fought with parents and/or practitioners when being left or collected?
- tried to run out of the setting?
- refused to be comforted?
- withdrew from others?
- chose to play with the same activity or stay in the same area day after day?
- refused to join in group activities?
- dawdled, hung back when asked to move from one area or activity to another?
- dissociated, switched off from their surroundings?
- displayed a mix – or even all – of these behaviours?

Thinking back, is it possible that the stress of separation, or change of any kind during the day, may have contributed to the behaviour?

does fear (Whalen 2007; Jensen 2011). Uncertainty inevitably plays a big part in transition and, in the right conditions, has an important function in learning and adaptation. It is linked to curiosity, investigation and 'finding out' about new situations. If everything was 'certain', we wouldn't need to hypothesise, or experiment or investigate.

A calm, regulated child can respond to uncertainty with curiosity and interest, wondering what will happen next and feeling ready for it. For a child who is already anxious, uncertainty may trigger increased amygdala activity and shut down other cognitive processes, like the urge to investigate or experiment, because the uncertainty seems to pose too much of a threat to allow new learning.

Concerns about daycare

Armed with the information from these first two chapters about the impact of separation on young children, it is reasonable to ask questions about the prominent role that 'daycare' (childcare outside the home) has come to have in our society. Richard Bowlby has voiced his concerns in his paper *The need for secondary attachments in daycare* and elsewhere. The paper is available to read on the website for the charity What About the Children? (www.whataboutthechildren.org.uk). You can also hear him talk about this in four short videos available to view online at YouTube (search for 'Secure Attachment and the Key Person in Daycare'; accessed 13 February 2012).

Bowlby describes the impact of impersonal care on young children, pointing out that children will have different ways of displaying their stress and anxiety in settings where the interactions are not warm, consistent and attuned to the individual child (R. Bowlby). Some will act out their distress aggressively, with hyperactivity or challenging and attention-seeking behaviour. Others will be more passive, appearing self-reliant and to be 'coping' as they resist comfort from adults in general, or seem 'happy' to accept help from any available adult. Without an understanding of attachment theory and brain development, both types of behaviour mask the stress and unhappiness of separation. One child may be judged as 'naughty' or difficult, because they are acting out their distress in challenging ways, while the other is seen as 'good' and settled, because they are not causing problems.

Once we know and understand a little more about attachment and how our brains work, we can begin to see that both children are communicating their distress – and both of them need the sensitive understanding and responses of a secure secondary attachment figure while they are away from home. These children present perfect examples of the way that degrees of insecure attachment can be expressed differently.

Although this is not a clinical description of attachment, I find it helpful to think of it as a swinging pendulum. The closer the pendulum swings to secure, the less marked the behaviour. As it swings way out from secure it becomes more extreme. Can you see the links here with the primitive fight, flight or freeze response? The aggressive acting out and attention-seeking behaviours are linked to the 'fight' reaction, while the more passive and over-compliant behaviours arise from the instinct for flight (avoidance) and freeze (surrender) becoming distant, removed and dissociated.

Both types of children are harmed by the experience. One may be labelled difficult and find themselves constantly punished and rebuked for 'bad' behaviour and poor discipline. The other may appear on the face of it to reap all the benefits of being 'good' and compliant, but these children also display less curiosity and risk taking, and may have a lack of interest in creative and social play, which has a detrimental effect on their cognitive and social development. Both children are living with high levels of stress, which we know can have a profound impact on their physical and emotional health.

Furthermore, as Richard Bowlby points out, a child with insecure attachments at home, who is then left with impersonal daycare providers, is in a 'double risk' situation.

> Toddlers who are *insecurely* attached to their primary attachment figure have a risk factor. Toddlers who are *securely* attached may have a risk factor if they are in non-parental daycare without an attachment figure. These two risk factors are difficult to detect *individually*, but if toddlers are both insecurely attached *and* have no access to an attachment figure during daycare, they experience two risk factors which acting together are likely to be more easily noticed.
>
> (R. Bowlby 2007; emphasis in original)

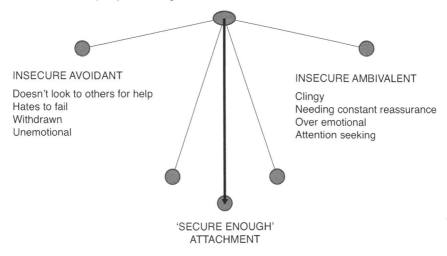

INSECURE DISORGANISED
aggression, dissociation, resisting attachment, indiscriminate attachment,
lack of empathy, controlling behaviour, failure to thrive, anti-social behaviour

INSECURE AVOIDANT

Doesn't look to others for help
Hates to fail
Withdrawn
Unemotional

INSECURE AMBIVALENT

Clingy
Needing constant reassurance
Over emotional
Attention seeking

'SECURE ENOUGH'
ATTACHMENT

FIGURE 3 The swinging 'pendulum' of attachment.

We must remember too that a securely attached child is also at risk if they join a setting where the quality of sensitive attunement is poor. These children 'can develop an insecure attachment style as a means of coping with an unpredictable and inconsistent environment' (Read 2010:39), which can undo all the positive experiences of the home.

Sue Gerhardt considers the impact of impersonalised care in her book *The Selfish Society: How we all forgot to love one another and made money instead* (2010). She takes issue with government's tacit approval of nursery provision for children under two, and suggests that 'a few months of good "bonding" which are then followed by a period in mass-produced, low-grade "care-giving" are not likely to give a baby the most favourable start in life' (Gerhardt 2010:330). She quotes Penelope Leach, who suggests that secondary attachment figures can provide the 'emotional life raft' that a child separated from their parents needs but then comments that 'some childcare experiences don't provide much of a raft at all' (Gerhardt 2010:332). This is a sad and deeply troubling fact that needs to be acknowledged by the profession – and by the corporate bodies and individuals who profit from poor-quality childcare. Where the quality of care is good, she does acknowledge that the situation can be less damaging: 'Of course, if they have good enough childcare during the day (particularly if they are given the chance to form meaningful ongoing attachments) and then come home to sensitive, loving and attentive parents, they are just as likely to develop the capacity for secure attachment as a stay at home child' (Gerhardt 2010:331), but points out just how difficult it can be for tired parents who only spend a few short hours with their child, before and after work, to be able to tune in sensitively to their babies and young children when they have such a limited time with them.

The bottom line for Gerhardt (and others) would seem to be that as a society we should move away from impersonalised care for children under two and that the government should support parents to remain at home with their children and build those all important attachments that have such a bearing not only on the future well-being of their children, but on society as a whole. For children over two, some form of personalised care outside the home would seem to be acceptable and generally beneficial, but only if the care is of a high enough quality.

This is borne out by American research (cited by Gerhardt in her earlier book, *Why Love Matters*, 2004) that studied the cortisol levels of three- and four-year-olds in a day nursery. Cortisol levels rose during the day and were at their highest in the afternoon (a time when they would normally be sinking in children at home with a parent), even in children who did not appear to be stressed (Dettling, Gunnar and Donzella 1999). In a second study, the cortisol levels of children cared for by childminders were measured (Dettling, Parker, Lane, Sebanc and Gunnar 2000). Gerhardt describes how Dettling and colleagues 'found that what really mattered was the quality of the replacement caregiving and whether there was someone really paying attention to the child. Children who were placed with childminders who were highly responsive to them had normal cortisol levels' (Gerhardt 2004:74).

Sadly, despite lots of political championing of 'family values' and government initiatives claiming to support families with young children, no political party has yet to promise the kind of incentives that would encourage and allow parents to stay at home and support them in building secure attachments with their babies under two. But that doesn't mean that we shouldn't keep shouting about the need for it – and to insist that when care is required outside the home it must be high-quality, personalised and nurturing.

Positive interventions to support attachment

All this information about the crucial nature of a child's early experiences shouldn't prevent us from being hopeful about the impact of positive intervention for vulnerable children and their families. We have increasing information to suggest that the brain has 'plasticity' throughout life and that positive intervention that promotes attachment can make a big difference. As long ago as 1965, D.W. Winnicott was talking about 'second chance learning' – the 'opportunity to provide a new experience of consistent care through sensitive caregiving' (Read 2010:39).

Children's Centres have an important role to play in providing family support and outreach that focuses on improving the quality of attachment and relationship in vulnerable families. By providing targeted support for inexperienced, vulnerable and less resilient parents, through sessions promoting breastfeeding and baby massage as well as structured parenting courses highlighting the importance of nurture and relationships, Children's Centres build the confidence and raise the self-esteem of parents struggling with the day-to-day challenges of parenting.

Impact of attachment theory

Attachment theory has had a profound impact on the way children are cared for in hospitals. No longer is a parent expected to leave a young child alone in hospital for extended periods, and neo-natal wards caring for premature babies make every attempt to allow parents physical access to their babies, promoting as much early attachment as is possible.

But it seems to have taken a long time for attachment theory to filter through to the educational world. It features in training for teachers and childcare workers, along with all the other theories of child development, but hasn't been much in evidence in the daily life of the classroom, nor does it feature strongly in government policy or curriculum decisions. Recent developments in neuroscience seem to be confirming what Bowlby and others believed, and this will no doubt help to cause a shift in understanding eventually.

Charities and organisations such as What About the Children? (WATCh) help raise awareness of the emotional needs of children under three. Its website provides 'information from research for parents, professionals and policy makers, about the critical importance of secure primary attachment for healthy emotional development' (www.whataboutthechildren.org.uk).

Attachment theory remains a 'theory', however, and as such is subject to huge amounts of continuing debate. There is no doubt that we still have much to learn about the way the human race has evolved – and will continue to evolve – so we need to stay flexible and open-minded about what we have yet to learn. What we mustn't do is delay. There is enough evidence already to suggest that our current social climate is impacting negatively on the quality of attachment in many families and that too many early transitions are adding to the problem, particularly for our most vulnerable children.

Summary

This chapter aimed to provide just a brief exploration of some of the most important aspects of brain development that have a bearing on transitions. Hopefully, together with the information in Chapter 1, this has been helpful in explaining not just *how* our brains function, but also *why* we react in certain ways when faced with change and unfamiliar situations.

Our brains have evolved to keep us alive, to keep us safe, to recognise threat and to rationalise our response to it.

- We function best when all three parts – the reptilian, mammalian and rational brain – work together in combination.
- Young children's brains are not fully developed and so the lower 'instinctive' brain is mostly in charge.

- Young children's instinctive responses to a perceived threat can impact on their ability to learn.
- Warm, affectionate and attuned responses from adults help young children to:
  - regulate their instincts and emotions
  - create efficient pathways in their brain
  - increase the flow of feel-good hormones while regulating the levels of stress chemicals in their bodies
  - build positive patterns of behaviours.

Implications for our practice

With an increased understanding of brain development, we are better equipped to:

- use our current knowledge and understanding to inform our approaches to children's care and learning;
- be open to adapting our approaches as neuroscience increasingly unfolds new information about brain development;
- work with parents to support their understanding that love and unconditional affection are not just desirable, but are essential for brain development;
- use our professional judgement to challenge inappropriate transitions and poor-quality care.

3

A 'patchwork of services'
Why do young children experience so many transitions?

This chapter explores the history of how services and education for young children have developed in such a fragmented way, leading to so many potential transitions for babies and children up to the age of five and beyond. It also considers how research and theories about children's experience of transition can help us, as practitioners, to respond better to their needs while continuing to challenge the expectation that excessive transitions are normal – and acceptable – in a young child's life.

REFLECTION TASK

Have a think about . . . your own early experiences of childcare and education.

- How much do you remember about the process of starting school or nursery?
- What do you know about the history of early years provision in general and more specifically in your region?
- Why do you think there is so much academic interest and research into the way that young children deal with transitions?

A brief history of early years provision

> Nowhere in the United Kingdom has a universal system of early childhood services been established. We have instead a patchwork of provision that can be confusing for parents and inadequate to meet all needs.
>
> (Baldock 2011:130)

In the introduction to his book *Developing Early Childhood Services Past, Present and Future* (2011), Peter Baldock writes: 'The subject does not have the profile it might have. You could compile a quite respectable list of authoritative books covering between them the social history of our country over the last five hundred years and find the care and education of the youngest children rarely mentioned, if mentioned at all' (Baldock 2011:1). He suggests a possible explanation for this neglect. 'The care and education of children have usually been seen as the responsibility of mothers, and anything done by women who were not monarchs or other public figures failed until fairly recently to attract the interest of historians' (Baldock 2011:1).

Because of this lack of authoritative material and the disparate nature of the services involved, it is really quite difficult to give a step-by-step historical account of the process that has led to this 'patchwork of provision'. Added to this are the complex and significant variations in policy across countries within the United Kingdom. This is just a brief summary of some of the key aspects.

Childcare: a post-industrial concept?

Baldock describes how urbanisation has been the chief activator of change in the way that children are cared for. Previously, much of the population lived in rural communities and children were pretty much kept alongside the adults at all times, joining them in the fields and villages, both at work and at play.

Urbanisation came about largely as a result of the Industrial Revolution. 'The change to an urbanised and industrialised society in the nineteenth century was rapid. By the 1840s the urban population of England was twice the size of the rural one' (Baldock 2011:2). Child labour was common and the move towards education for the working classes was, in part, a humane response to challenging this practice as well as a religious or moral concern to provide 'training in disciplined obedience' for the masses (Whitbread 1972:5). There was little differentiation for the needs of the very youngest, although there is evidence of nurseries being provided for the children of mothers working in factories from as early as 1835 (Baldock 2011:11) – the problems of financial sustainability were as relevant then as they are to this day. The fees were often too high to be affordable to the families who needed the childcare most, and so the nurseries closed.

'Dame schools' were another alternative in the early 1800s and can be described as 'mutual self-help arising within working class culture in the early industrial era' (Whitbread 1972:7). A woman (usually elderly) in the neighbourhood would take as many children as she could into her own home and charge for their care and sometimes a modicum of education depending on her own literacy levels. An early form of childminding that was unlikely in most cases to provide quality in care or education.

But the issues of daycare were seen as separate to the desire for infant education. In 1804 Joseph Lancaster had started his 'monitorial system' of schooling for the working classes, where large numbers of children of all ages could be taught together, with older children acting as 'monitors'. When a split occurred in

The Lancasterian Society (founded by Lancaster to promote his system), his influence declined and other members of the society went on to develop more schools. Samuel Wilderspin in particular set up infant schools designed to include very young children.

The government of 1846 oversaw the replacement of the monitorial system with one where 'pupil teachers' (older pupils) worked in a form of apprenticeship, and in 1862 the government introduced a system of paying schools grants based on results.

1870–1945

'The social, economic and political changes that happened around the year 1870 affected services for young children. In the seventy years or so that followed, the foundations were laid for government to take the lead role in education, including early education and for the provision of new services in daycare, child protection, playwork and support to mothers' (Baldock 2011:24).

This was good, but also saw the beginnings of the 'fragmentation' we live with today. Areas other than schooling are identified as being important in the welfare of children, and the other agencies and professions described above by Baldock begin to emerge. Children's health, in particular, is of increasing concern.

A system of Elementary Schools was created by the 1870 Education Act, and in 1871 the teaching requirements of children aged five to seven became distinct from those for older children, although many schools continued to cater for children under five years of age. By 1876 education for children under the age of 10 had become compulsory.

Here is where we first see the notion that formal schooling should begin at the age of five. The rest of Europe continued to believe it should take place around the eighth year, and even within Britain the privately educated child wouldn't begin 'preparatory' school until later. 'The decision to make the fifth rather than the seventh birthday the boundary point was not taken on grounds related to any theory of education. It seems to have been based on the view that the sooner the children of the working class had concluded elementary education and were ready for employment, the better (Blackstone 1971:23).

Regardless of the rights and wrongs of setting a starting age of five (and we will return to this, as it is a significant factor in young children's experience of transitions in the UK), the reality was that lots of children were actually in school long before they reached their fifth birthday. Working class parents had plenty of reasons for wanting their youngest children safely inside a school building with their older siblings, whether or not they were interested in their education. This proved to be a problem for the authorities, who attempted to refuse admission to under-fives in the already overcrowded schools.

Kindergartens and nursery schools

Meanwhile, in middle class areas another development was taking place. The kindergarten (for children aged two to seven years) was pioneered by Friedrich Froebel (1782–1852) in Germany and the movement spread to the established German communities in Manchester and London. From the Froebelian model emerged much of what we recognise today as good practice. Other pioneers include Maria Montessori, Rudolf Steiner, Susan Isaacs and Margaret McMillan. McMillan built on the Froebelian model to develop the 'British nursery school' which she believed should be 'an extension of, not substitute for, home' (Bruce, Meggitt and Grenier 2010:445). Isaacs, Steiner and McMillan believed that children should stay in a nursery-type environment until the age of seven. Other common beliefs among these pioneers was the emphasis placed on relationships, play and involving parents.

Nursery education or compensatory daycare?

'The British nursery school, as envisaged by McMillan, has been admired and emulated across the world' (Bruce et al. 2010:445). Despite this, and the growing support for these schools in the early part of the twentieth century, they have never become universally available across the country. In the economic crisis after the First World War, initiatives for under-fives were stifled although the Nursery School Association (NSA) was set up in 1923 to campaign for a commitment to separate pre-school provision. The new Labour Government of 1929 promised expansion; when this didn't happen, some local authorities developed nursery classes within elementary schools, although this wasn't widespread (Baldock 2011:32).

Along with the lack of economic and financial will to promote nursery education for all, there was another factor working against the development of universal provision. Helen Bilton explores the historical perspective of nursery education in her book *Outdoor Play in the Early Years: Management and Innovation* (2002), and describes how the success of McMillan and others in raising awareness of the importance of children's physical health may have inadvertently led to the downgrading of nursery provision. 'In a sense, the nursery movement's success was also its downfall. As nursery education was seen to dramatically improve the health of children, the conclusion drawn by some was that nursery education was not a new type of education but simply a compensatory education. Put poor, disease ridden children in the nursery and they will get healthier' (Bilton 2002:28). The health-giving properties of nurseries were largely attributed to the emphasis on outdoor play and the nursery garden. Bilton also draws links here with differing perspectives on infant and nursery provision, noting that the garden was not seen as integral to the learning environment but was there purely 'as a health promoting environment' (Bilton 2002:28).

Infant education, however, took place indoors in classrooms, and though the tables and chairs might have been child-sized and suitable for 'play' activities, the furniture was there for the purpose of sitting at and 'learning'. Playtime happened in the playground (usually a bare expanse of hard ground bound by high walls or railings) at restricted times. There still exists a debate about the supposed differences between the concepts of early education, the provision of daycare and the need to provide compensatory experiences for young, underprivileged children.

1960s and 1970s

At the beginning of the 1960s nursery provision was far from universal and 'few children were offered more than a few hours a week of group care before they started school' (Brooker 2008:23). The nursery schools that had opened during the Second World War had mostly closed following the end of the war, and only those who could afford it paid for private nursery school. Social Services nurseries existed only for children considered to be at risk and who met certain criteria that made them eligible for free daycare.

In 1961 Belle Tutaev, a young mother frustrated at the lack of state nursery provision, set up a group of her own. She discovered that many other parents across the UK were similarly frustrated and by 1962, the Pre-school Playgroups Association was in existence. Now known as the Pre-school Learning Alliance, it describes on its website the impact of this development.

> It soon became apparent however that the new charity and its groups were not merely remedying the lack of state nursery provision; they were accomplishing something much more. The direct involvement and empowerment of the children's own parents had a powerful effect not only on the children's learning but also on the parents themselves:
>
> - Children learn better when their parents are involved. Seeing their own families validated and powerful gives them a secure base from which to progress, and parents who feel part of the pre-school are in a better position to reinforce at home the learning which has occurred in the group.
> - Adults who discover, as children do, that 'I can do it myself' become confident partners in the world of education rather than mere consumers. In addition to the advantages this offers the child – and any subsequent children – it can also extend personal and educational development for the parents themselves. 40,000 adults a year were attending Pre-school Learning Alliance courses, many of them going on to further training and career developments.
>
> (www.pre-school.org.uk/about-us/history)
> (accessed 5 February 2012)

This awareness of the importance of parental involvement and engagement has spread across all areas of education as well as the early years. The playgroup movement was very significant in the development of early years provision and the Pre-school Learning Alliance continues to play an important campaigning role.

Nursery classes and nursery schools

The falling birth rate of the 1970s led to empty classrooms in infant and primary schools being used to create nursery classes for three- and four-year-olds. Not only did this impact on the viability of some playgroups, it also affected in some instances the suitability of the environment both indoors and out. Inevitably, some of the earlier 'health promoting' elements of outdoor nursery provision became lost as nursery education was seen increasingly 'as a solution to educational disadvantage', preparing children for compulsory schooling and identifying special needs (Bilton 2002:28). However, in my experience of infant and nursery teaching from the late 1970s onwards, many practitioners in maintained nursery classes continued to draw their inspiration from the British nursery schools approach, ensuring high-quality experiences for children, indoors and out, that were not purely to prepare them for school.

The current information provided for parents on the government website (www.direct.gov.uk) explains that:

> Nursery classes and schools fall into two groups – state and private. Most day nurseries are privately run. Most nurseries:
>
> - will take your child between the ages of three and five, although many day nurseries take younger children
> - open throughout the school year, although some private day nurseries open during the school holidays
> - operate a core day of 9.00 am to 3.30 pm, although many nurseries offer longer days
> - offer five half-day sessions, although some types of nursery will offer part-time or full-time places depending on your needs
>
> Nursery schools and classes have a minimum ratio of two adults to 20 to 26 children. One must be a qualified teacher, the other a qualified nursery assistant.
>
> Day nurseries have more intensive staffing ratios and different rules on qualifications of staff depending on the ages of children being cared for.
>
> (www.direct.gov.uk/en/Parents/Preschooldevelopmentandlearning/
> NurseriesPlaygroupsReceptionClasses/DG_10013534)
> (accessed 9 February 2012)

Childminders

The following is just a brief summary of the history of childminding, adapted from an article on the website *Registered Childminding* (www.childminding-success.co.uk) that describes the developments from the unregulated 'baby farms' in the early days of the industrial revolution to the current day, when childminders are acknowledged in the Early Years Foundation Stage (EYFS) framework on an equal footing with other childcare settings.

Childminders were brought under local authority control for the first time in 1948 as a result of the Nurseries and Childminders Act, though the regulations were minimal. Training was not thought to be required, nor were there any inspections. Regulations were not significantly increased until the 1989 Children Act, although responsibility for registering childminders changed in 1974 from Local Health Authorities to Social Services departments. In 1977 The National Childminding Association (NCMA) was formed as childminders sought to improve standards, raise their profile and obtain better support. Standardisation of quality of care was introduced in 2001 when Ofsted became the regulator for childcare in England, providing registration and inspection. Childminders were also required to take a training course and be checked by the Criminals Records Bureau. Childminders were supported by the Birth to Three Matters framework (2002), and their professional status began to be acknowledged as the public became aware of the increased legislation and training involved in being a childminder (www.childminding-success.co.uk/business/history-of-childminding).

The NCMA's website (www.ncma.org.uk) states its belief that children of all ages benefit from home-based childcare, play and learning because it is:

- **consistent** – a child is cared for by the same registered childminder or nanny each day, often over a number of years
- **flexible** – for example, a registered childminder or nanny can care for a child whose parents work atypical hours and will provide full, as well as wraparound, childcare
- **inclusive** – a registered childminder or nanny can care for children of different ages and abilities together in family groups
- **community-focused** – a registered childminder or nanny can reflect the needs of local communities and enable the children they care for to be part of their local community
- **personalised** – a registered childminder or nanny can meet the needs of individual children and families, such as teen parents or disabled children
- **supportive** – babies and younger children, especially, do best in home-based childcare because they are cared for in smaller groups and by the same registered childminder or nanny each day (www.ncma.org.uk/about_ncma.aspx) (accessed 5 February 2012).

Elinor Goldschmied and Sonia Jackson, the authors of *People under Three: Young children in daycare* are also clear about the superior value of childminders:

> On balance we think home-based care is better adapted to the needs of babies than a group setting, provided the childminder understands that her role goes far beyond physical caring. Good care by one person is almost certain to be more loving and sensitive than care by a number of different people, however competent.
>
> (Goldschmied and Jackson 1994:74)

More recent developments in policy and practice in early years provision

The last 20–30 years have seen an unprecedented amount of change and policy directives that have had a direct impact on early years provision. The Education Reform Act (1988) introduced a National Curriculum from the age of five, while the Children Act (1989) began the process of bringing together under one legislation all services relating to children from birth to eight. The Early Excellence Centre Programme (DfEE 1997) and the introduction of Sure Start (DfEE 1998) – 'an early intervention programme for young children under the age of 4 years in areas of high deprivation in the UK' (Page and Nutbrown 2008:43) – focused on meeting local needs through a range of services. The National Childcare Strategy (1998) stressed the importance of parental choice and proposed a range of childcare options including maintained nursery schools and classes, private daycare, voluntary playgroups, childminding networks and wraparound care in extended schools and after-school clubs. Quite a dizzying array of options for those parents in a position to actually make a choice!

Children's Centres

Baldock tells how in 1943, the National Society of Children's Nurseries argued 'not only for a comprehensive system of nurseries after the war, but also for attaching "mothercraft centres" to them' (Baldock 2011:42, citing Nathan 1943). Although nothing came of these proposals at the time, it is proof that the idea of attaching parent support to daycare provision has been around for a long while. In 2002 the Inter-departmental Childcare Review (Sure Start 2002) suggested Children's Centres as the best way of providing a range of universal services to local communities (Page and Nutbrown 2008).

Archived content from the Department for Children, Schools and Families' (DCSF) 'Every Child Matters Homepage' on the National Archives shows a relatively recent perspective on Sure Start Children's Centres, describing them as service hubs where families of children under five receive 'seamless integrated services and information':

These services vary according to centre but may include:

- integrated early education and childcare – all centres offering Early Years provision have a minimum half-time qualified teacher (increasing to full-time within 18 months of the centre opening)
- support for parents – including advice on parenting, local childcare options and access to specialist services for families
- child and family health services – ranging from health screening, health visitor services to breast-feeding support
- helping parents into work – with links to the local Jobcentre Plus and training.

> (http://webarchive.nationalarchives.gov.uk/20100113205508/dcsf.
> gov.uk/everychildmatters/earlyyears/surestart/surestartchildrens
> centres/childrenscentres) (accessed 13 February 2012)

Many children's centres offer high-quality drop-in sessions promoting play and other activities designed to foster good attachments within families as well as children's physical, emotional, social and intellectual development. Children's centres attached to nursery and primary schools, in particular, are well placed to support children's transitions into education by providing strong links and family support for vulnerable families. There are also good examples of stand-alone children's centres forging good relationships with local childcare providers and feeder schools, supporting families with transition into reception classes. Since the change in government in 2010, however, the future of Children's Centres has seemed uncertain.

The Foundation Stage and the EYFS

The emergence of the Foundation Stage saw the three to five age group declared as a separate educational entity with its own *Curriculum Guidance for the Foundation Stage* (DfEE 2000) and was followed in 2002 by the launch of *Birth to Three Matters: A Framework to Support Children in their Earliest Years* (DfES 2002). These were superseded by the Early Years Foundation Stage (DfES 2006), which combined the two to produce a new curriculum framework that became statutory for funded provision from birth to five (Page and Nutbrown 2008:46). Although many believe that the existence of the frameworks has improved the regulation and consistency of early years provision, there remain some very serious concerns about the formal nature of the EYFS curriculum and its impact, particularly on babies.

The Tickell Review (2011) proposed a slimmed-down framework and assessment, with the revised EYFS scheduled for September 2012. Early years specialists, practitioners, parents and other interested bodies continue to voice concern over the narrow and prescriptive nature of the guidance, the inappropriateness of some of the developmental guidelines and the disregard for early years pedagogy. These issues all have a bearing on the way transitions are handled as they can influence settings to adopt inappropriate practice in the drive to meet generalised milestones and benchmarks.

Free education places for three-year-olds and four-year-olds

Currently in England and Wales all three- and four-year-olds are entitled to a free early education place during term time (15 hours a week spread flexibly), although parents are not obliged to use it. This may be in nursery schools, nursery classes in primary schools, playgroups, private or independent nurseries or with childminders registered with an approved network, though not all providers take part in the scheme (www.adviceguide.org.uk/index/your_family/education/access_to_education.htm#compulsory_school_age). In 2011 the government announced its intention to extend this to include around 40% of two-year-olds by 2014–15, with eligibility criteria targeting disadvantaged families (www.education.gov.uk/childrenandyoungpeople/earlylearningandchildcare/delivery/Free%20Entitlement%20to%20Early%20Education/b0070114/elfordisadvantaged).

SEN and inclusion

Until relatively recently, children considered to have special needs with regard to their health, learning or behaviour were educated outside of mainstream provision. For some children, this would begin in the early years in specialist nurseries; for others it would involve a transition from mainstream to special school once their needs had been recognised and formally assessed. The development of policies for inclusive education and the provision of greater specialist support within mainstream have reduced some of the problematic transition experiences for these children.

Children who attend special schools, often outside their neighbourhood, need to be transported by bus and usually from a young age. This adds another layer of transition to their day and generally removes the parent from the daily settling process, as well as reducing the possibility of carrying local friendships into school with them. Although inclusive education has not been without its challenges, when it is well resourced I believe it to be beneficial for all. This is for a wealth of reasons, not least of which is the opportunity it provides to reduce the transitions experienced by vulnerable children with special needs.

Compulsory school age

As already mentioned, the school starting age has not changed since the early days of compulsory schooling. R. Szretzer wrote a fascinating paper in 1964 in the *British Journal for Educational Studies* entitled 'The Origins of Compulsory Schooling for Five Year Olds', in which he explored the arbitrary reasons why the age for starting school was set at five years and challenged the notion that it should be allowed to continue without question.

Szretzer describes the view of W.E. Forster (Minister of Education in 1870) that compulsory schooling would improve the lot of the children of the working class poor: 'A hundred years ago almost any form of schooling, at however low an age, was fundamentally in the interest of the type of child Forster had in mind. It afforded him protection from the street, from the factory, or from the drudgery and comprehensive poverty of his home.' But then he adds: 'Today we should perhaps consider whether the 4-year and 5-year-old child should not be to some extent protected from the school' (Szretzer 1964:28). Almost 50 years later, early years experts continue to question the validity of such an early school start, and readily express their concerns about the need to 'protect' children from the 'too much, too soon' school experience (House 2011).

Interestingly, although government ideas about when education should start don't seem to have changed, they have dramatically shifted the age at which children should leave school. We now anticipate by 2015 a school leaving age of 18. That's eight long years more than in 1870! Yet the government in the UK continues to hold fast to the idea of five as a suitable age to start formal schooling. Baldock comments that 'there is little stomach anywhere in the political system for challenging the daft decision of 1870 to treat the fifth birthday as a crucial boundary point for education, even though the original motive behind that decision (that politicians wanted young people to get out to work as soon as possible) has disintegrated with frequent changes in the school leaving age since then' (Baldock 2011:131).

The legal age for the start of compulsory schooling continues to be the term after a child's fifth birthday, but the reality is that, just as in the early days of elementary education, many children actually start school well before they are five, because of the once a year point of admission now generally used by local authorities. Although parents are entitled to delay the start of school until the term after their child is five, they are generally reluctant to do so for fear of losing the school place of their choice, or of their child 'missing out' on time spent in school or being isolated from friendship groups already established.

The academic year and the 'summer born child'

The academic year begins in September. There are currently three school terms: Autumn, Spring and Summer. These more or less match the historical division of the year practised at Oxford University (Michaelmas, Hilary and Trinity) from where the practice may have derived. Until fairly recently, many local authorities organised the reception class intake around three points of entry – September, January and April – at the start of each school term, with children generally beginning school in the term in which their fifth birthday occurred. This was described as 'rising five'. Depending on the size of the school yearly intake, this might mean creating a full reception class each term of children closely grouped in age, or more commonly, 'growing' a class by adding 10–12 children each term.

Either way, this has meant that the oldest children have three terms in reception and the youngest just one. In times (and areas) of teacher shortage (e.g. London in the 1980s) some authorities chose to revert temporarily to the 'legal five' starting point, and so the summer born children missed out the reception class completely and went straight into 'middle infants' (Y1). Although the provision once they arrived in school may not always have been appropriately matched to their needs, it did mean that children stayed in nursery or at home until a slightly later age.

The debate about single or multiple points of entry into school

If all the children who will turn five sometime in that academic year begin school together in September, then it is possible to have two children in the same class celebrating their birthdays on consecutive days. One will be five on 1 September; the other will have only just turned four the previous day, on 31 August. This has considerable implications for developmentally appropriate teaching.

But the situation was no more straightforward before the single point of entry in September became more widespread. Previously, the diversity in provision across the country meant that a four-year-old in one area would be classified as a 'nursery age child' while another four-year-old born on the same day in a different part of the country would be considered to be of 'reception age'. Most people with early years expertise would consider the four-year-old in the nursery to be the fortunate one, whereas less well-informed government ministers, the media and ultimately parents, might be forgiven for assuming that the child getting into school earlier is in the better position. And certainly, this has been the thrust of much of the concern in the past about 'summer born' children who are seen to be missing out on time spent in school. There is no easy answer to this problem, as the solution to have each child begin school (or nursery) individually around the date of their birthday could be just as fraught with complexity!

Liz Brooker explores this issue in her book *Supporting Transitions in the Early Years*: 'The important question, however, may not be "when do they start?" but "what do they start?"' She draws comparisons between the informal reception classes some of us may have experienced in the 1960s and 1970s – 'days spent in singing, stories and free play, in and out of doors' and the reception classes of the early twenty-first century, which, 'despite their mandatory outdoor curriculum, may make far greater demands on young children' (Brooker 2008:28).

School readiness

Brooker also points out that government policy-makers tend to view children's transitions purely in terms of 'school readiness'. Writing in 2008 about the USA and Australia, she comments on how

> transition strategies have concentrated on the concept of readiness, generally in the traditional sense of the 'readiness for school' of each individual child. The burden of responsibility for a successful transition in this view, lies with the child and with those adults whose task it is to prepare her or him for 'stepping up' the educational ladder. Successful transitions, in this account, are achieved by individuals who have acquired the requisite academic knowledge and social skills to perform, conform and *learn* in the new setting. This perspective which tends to blame those children, families and communities who have not achieved readiness, was exemplified in the first of the US *National Educational Goals* ('by the year 2000 all children in America will start school ready to learn'; National Education Goals Panel 1991) although it has been repeatedly critiqued by researchers.
>
> (Brooker 2008:5–6; emphasis in original)

Given that school readiness is now a major focus of the UK government and its revised framework for the EYFS, it is worth spending a little bit of time in 'critiquing' this notion ourselves. In this case, being 'ready' for the next stage is not based on moving a child on when the time is right and they are 'ready, willing and able' (Carr 2001) to make the most of what comes next. Instead it is about expectations of a set of 'achievements' (i.e. skills and abilities) that a child is considered to need in order not to slow down the 'work' of the next stage. Put crudely – and extending the 'blame' onto the workforce – this implies that the next practitioner shouldn't have to spend time working on something the previous practitioner was supposed to have taught the child.

The first *Curriculum Guidance for the Foundation Stage* (DfEE 2000) stated very clearly that the early years were a stage in themselves – they were not 'preparation' for something more important that came after. Despite this continuing to be a firmly held principle in early years pedagogy, it would appear that it is still not embedded in the understanding of policy-makers. Most early years practitioners would also take exception to the implication in Brooker's quote that learning only begins once the child reaches school!

Even though we know that for most of our children, starting school is no longer the first transitional milestone from home that it once was, it still carries a lot of weight and meaning in our society. Being 'ready for school' implies that it is the child (and their family) that have to do all the work and make all the changes. Writing in *Informing Transitions in the Early Years: Research, policy and practice* (Dunlop and Fabian 2007), Sue Dockett and Bob Perry note that 'In general, as children start school there is a clear expectation that they will change and change considerably. In other words, the expectation is that the least experienced participants in the transition – the children – will change the most' (Dockett and Perry 2007:98).

But researchers are beginning to suggest that we need to also ask the question 'Is this school ready for this child?' (Niesel and Griebel in Dunlop and Fabian 2007:25). Bearing in mind the individual needs of all children, this sounds like a tall order. But I would like to suggest that an increase in our understanding of early child development, and the way in which attachments support resilience, will go a long way in helping us to be 'child ready', at whatever age the transition process takes place.

Differences across the UK

The subtle switch from 'early years' to formal schooling is, to a certain extent, viewed differently in countries of the UK other than England. Julie Fisher provides a very useful account of the differences in her book, *Moving on to Key Stage One: Improving Transition from the Early Years Foundation Stage* (2010) as she explores the ways in which Wales and Scotland recognise the value of not separating education for three- to five-year-olds from the provision for five- to seven-year-old children.

In Wales, the Foundation Phase (introduced by the Welsh Assembly in 2008) begins at age three and continues to the end of Key Stage 1, when children are seven years old. A principle of the Foundation Stage Framework for Children's Learning for 3–7 year olds in Wales (DCELLS 2008) is that 'a curriculum for young children should be appropriate to their stage of learning rather than focusing solely on age-related outcomes to be achieved' (Fisher 2010:34; DCELLS 2008:4). Scotland's Curriculum for Excellence also challenges 'over-emphasis on systematic teaching before 6 or 7 years of age', and encourages active learning with an emphasis on the quality of interactions and relationships (Fisher 2010:34).

International perspectives

A great deal is written about the comparative differences in compulsory school age around the world. The most striking aspect is just how far England differs from the majority of European countries, where compulsory schooling does not begin until age six at the earliest, and in several countries not until age seven. There would appear to be no clear evidence that starting school earlier provides any academic advantage and as Julie Fisher, among many other commentators, reminds us, 'What matters most of all is not the age at which children start school, but whether their experiences once they are *in* school are appropriate to their age and stage of development' (Fisher 2010:36; emphasis in original). The impact of transition at a young age is potentially devastating when children enter a world that is radically different to the one they are leaving and that doesn't take their individual needs and experience levels into account.

Bronfenbrenner

Thinking about the contrast in the 'worlds' that children may experience brings us to the work of Urie Bronfenbrenner (1917–2005), often referred to as the 'father of transition studies' (Brooker 2008:5). His major work, *The Ecology of Human Development* (1979), describes 'the human individual as a participant in an array of inter-locking "systems", all of which have an impact, either direct or indirect, on his or her development' (Brooker 2008:20).

Liz Brooker provides a relatively simple explanation of this complex idea.

> Each setting the child experiences – home, childminder's house, granny's house, nursery or school – is described as a 'microsystem', and each of these has a role to play in the child's development. But Bronfenbrenner argues that the most important contribution to a child's well-being is the set of links between the *microsystems* – which he calls a *mesosystem*. Basically, the more links there are, and the stronger these links are, the better the child's experience and outcomes are likely to be.
>
> (Brooker 2008:21; emphasis in original)

She suggests how these links might look in practice:

- informal meetings between parents and teachers/practitioners
- home visits
- parents spending time in the setting
- information from home to setting – about the child's routines, preferences etc.
- information from setting to home – from teachers/practitioners about routines, plans etc.

- familiar objects from home or setting going back and forth (e.g. child's toy, comforter, book bag etc.)

- presence of familiar person (adult or child) during the settling process

This last one is particularly important. Bronfenbrenner makes the point that a transition has more developmental potential 'if the person's initial transition into that setting is not made alone, that is, if he enters the new setting in the company of one or more persons with whom he has participated in prior settings (for example, the mother accompanies the child to school)' (Bronfenbrenner 1979:211).

But, as Brooker points out, that link won't be sufficient if transition is viewed just as a one-off event. 'When children are young, it may seem as if the "transition" from one microsystem to another takes place daily, or at least weekly and is felt especially acutely after a break or holiday, so the supportive links between home and school need to be constantly available, and constantly renewed' (Brooker 2008:21). This is such an important feature of a successful approach to transitions, yet one that is constantly overlooked.

Horizontal and vertical transitions

Transitions aren't only about the milestones on the way to starting school. We define those as the *vertical* transitions that might take place at different stages – and ages – in a young child's life. There are also likely to be many *horizontal* transitions just in the course of an average day in a young child's life. Liz Brooker describes the child as not just 'stepping up' the ladder to the next stage of schooling, but also 'stepping sideways' (Brooker 2008:25) through the different elements of possible provision that they and their family might have to experience. Drawing on findings from the EPPE (Effective Provision of Pre-school Education) project, she writes:

> Parents who needed to work or study were frequently obliged to make complicated arrangements for their young children's care: off early in the morning to a relative or childminder, and then on again into a half-day nursery or pre-school; back to the childminder, out to a toddler group, and back to the childminder or relative to await the parent's return. Even if each of the settings a child experiences is suitable and appropriate, safe and secure, the child's cumulative experience of changes, within the day or within the week, is both unplanned and unprecedented.
>
> (Brooker 2008:25)

Elinor Goldschmied and Sonia Jackson explored the impact of daily horizontal transitions when they occurred *even within the same setting*. They describe how a baby or young child might have their personal care needs met by a variety of different people during one day. Not only is it distressing being fed and changed by a different person each time, it also means that all the wonderful bonding and opportunities for intimacy that feeding and personal care routines can bring are completely wasted. They likened it to adults experiencing multiple serial care when in hospital.

> We know from any hospital experience we may have had that a series of strange hands and different voices imposes great stress on us, especially when we are in a state of dependency, as young children always are.
>
> (Goldschmied and Jackson 1994:40)

This awareness has led to the development of the key person approach, something that has since been adopted by governmental early years guidance (DCSF 2008) but is not necessarily well understood. Chapter 5 looks at the key person approach in more depth.

The dangers of a 'pick and mix' approach to childcare and education?

Dorothy Y. Selleck addressed this question of multiple horizontal transitions in an article for *Early Education* (the journal of the British Association for Early Childhood Education) written in 2006.

> It is not enough to have principles for joined up working across the settings which children attend for different parts of the day (DfES 2006). Instead, we must support and inform parents to make the choice of *one* setting for their child that best meets their family's work/home arrangements. If the child's needs for key close attachments comes first then 'pick and mix' is not an option. It may suit us, the adults to join up the patches of services into a colourful blanket of different old wools, tensions and weaves – of crèches, playgroups, nursery classes, childminders, after school care, and daycare . . . [but, as Selleck points out with passion] if we do this then we are not putting the children in our settings first.
>
> (Selleck 2006:13)

Selleck goes on to confirm what I hope is a strong message throughout this book.

> Transitions and new people in our lives are not a 'bad idea' in themselves – there are times when we can all benefit from fresh relationships and new challenges, but for babies and young children this is not desirable. If broken attachments and serial carers are to be the norm then we are disregarding all we know about the importance of stable, healthy, secure relationships with just a few special people to nurture children's wellbeing, health and dispositions for learning.
>
> (Selleck 2006:13)

As with so many issues relating to education, health and social care, as a society we seem to accept a status quo that clearly has limitations, just because 'it's always been like that' or because it seems too complex to change. As pointed out in Chapter 2, in describing the development of childcare strategies arising from the motivations of industrialisation and capitalism, Gerhardt puts a clear case for not promoting impersonalised childcare for babies under two years old. Selleck is equally forceful in reminding us that merely advocating for 'smooth transitions' fudges the issue. We have to stop 'pretending' that the current situation of multiple transitions is acceptable and advocate 'for more energy focused on developing healthy key person attachments and less on multiple smooth transitions as we develop new policies and practice in the early years' (Selleck 2006:13).

Are seamless transitions possible?

To draw on both Baldock and Selleck's metaphor, then, this patchwork blanket might be a cosy 'wrap-around' cover that not only keeps out the draughts, but also is made in a bespoke fashion using familiar scraps and stitched with good intentions.

But there is no denying that these are scraps rather than quality lengths of fabric. They appear to fit together quite well, but they are not seamless. In fact they are full of stitched seams – and full of contrasts. Patchwork is never made exclusively from identical pieces of cloth. Why should it be? If you have enough quality cloth to make a blanket or quilt then there is no need to stitch pieces laboriously together, no matter how pretty it might look. As practitioners, however, we are urged to create smooth transitions – making the crossover from one provider to the next as 'seamless' as possible. But each one of our patchwork pieces of provision is stitched with a seam on all sides to connect it to the other pieces. None of it is seamless.

'A patchwork of provision'

Let's look at the vertical and horizontal transitions of three children aged five.

The child (and their family) in each example is at the centre, surrounded by the 'patches' of provision and attached by stitched seams. Some of these are 'horizontal' transitions and happen concurrently; for example, Tom moving between mum's friend, nursery, toddler group and crèche all in the same week. Other patches are 'vertical' transitions that occur consecutively as the child moves through the system. All of these different patches have their own different 'microsystem'. Some of those patches are linked to each other and have a seam in common (a 'mesosystem'), but others don't.

Where are the practitioners in this patchwork? Perhaps we are the 'thread' that holds the whole thing together? But if we take the analogy further, this thread needs to be strongly stitched and of the highest quality if the patchwork is not to fray and come apart – as it does for Laila. The EPPE study showed that the training and quality of practitioners working with young children is of particular

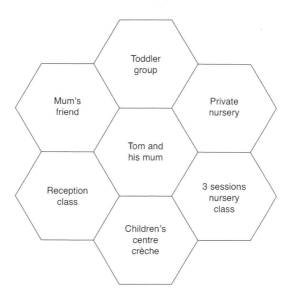

PATCHWORK 1 Tom lives with his mum, who works part-time. He was cared for in a private nursery and from the age of three he attended the local nursery class at the primary school. Mum's friend collected him from nursery on the days she worked late. On mum's days off he went to a toddler group and she used the crèche at the Children's Centre when she joined the parenting classes. He started school at age four years four months.

significance in the outcomes for children. Equally, the successful impact of the key person approach depends on the knowledge and understanding of practitioners as well as high levels of support and commitment from senior managers. But that all-important 'thread' that holds the patchwork together will be stretched to breaking point if:

- the status of those who work with young children continues to be low and the workforce does not include staff with teaching qualifications;
- good adult–child ratios are not maintained;
- the key person approach is not supported with adequate time, energy and resources to ensure its effectiveness;
- successive governments continue to over-prescribe the early years curriculum and attempt to drive practice with ill-judged targets and directives.

In an ideal world, a young child would spend most of the time bathed in unconditional love and affection with their secure and happy parents, and a small amount of time in the care of highly trained, well-paid professionals who love their job, and feel validated for the important work they do. Our world is far from ideal, however, and despite proclamations of support for families, current government policy and intervention continues to fail in interrupting what Gerhardt

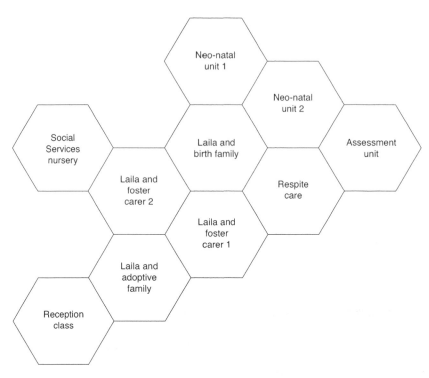

PATCHWORK 2 Laila was born 10 weeks prematurely to a teenage mother about to leave foster care. She was in a neo-natal care unit in one hospital for a week then moved to a hospital in another city where mum was provided with supported housing. She left hospital on her due date. A year later mum and baby were moved to a Social Services assessment unit following concerns about mum's ability to care for her. Laila was taken into respite care at age two and then placed with a long-term foster carer at age two years, three months. She was moved to another foster carer at age four and attended a full-time day nursery, prior to her adoption at age four years, six months. She started school at age four years, nine months.

(2010:334) calls 'intergenerational cycles of anxious attachment and inadequate emotional development'. But does that mean we must lose sight of the ideal?

Sue Gerhardt's challenge to the 'selfish society' is to 'build a culture and society which makes collective care a much higher priority – a more balanced culture which recognises that we have social needs as well as individual needs. These are the needs that we cannot meet individually – for shared facilities, for high quality housing in safe communities, for employment that allows employees time to raise their children as well as to enjoy other people's company' (Gerhardt 2010: 347–348). For now, we have to continue to fight to ensure that the needs of babies and young children are kept to the fore and that those of us currently involved in their care are well trained and well enough supported to be able to provide exactly what those children – and their parents – need from us.

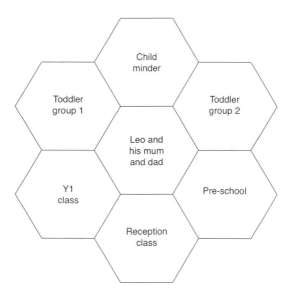

PATCHWORK 3 Leo lives with his mum and dad. Mum and dad shared childcare until he was two years, three months, when both returned to full-time work. He was then cared for by a childminder, who took him to two toddler groups. He started pre-school at three years, six months and entered reception at four years, five months. He transferred to Y1 at five years, five months.

Summary

This chapter aimed to provide a brief timeline of some of the major developments in early years policy and provision to give a sense of why, despite benefiting from some of the foremost thinking and practice in the field, we have arrived at such a fragmented structure within our early years provision.

- Urbanisation and the development of an industrialised society have been instrumental in the development of 'out of home' care for babies and young children.

- Early years provision in the UK has benefited from the theories and practice of a range of influential thinkers and activists.

- A wide range of factors have led to fragmentation in the provision of care and education for young children, which has normalised transitions to the point where they go unchallenged.

- The UK compulsory school starting age is merely historical and not based on any sound theories of learning or child development. It is not replicated in other European countries, where formal education does not begin until much later. Nor is it actually reflected in our own classrooms, where many children are in school when they are still only four.

- Notions of 'school readiness' continue to influence government policy and interventions.

- Babies and young children can potentially experience several 'horizontal' transitions of care during the day as well as 'vertical' transitions as they move through provision towards education.

- Bronfenbrenner's theories of transitions suggest that the well-being of a child who experiences several 'microsystems' of care is at risk if they do not have strong links between them.

- Where transitions continue to be inevitable, they are best supported by experienced, well-trained practitioners using a key person approach and working in close partnerships with the child's parents.

Implications for practice

An increased understanding of the historical background of fragmentation in early years services enables us to:

- challenge the continued existence of inappropriate practice and policies

- emphasise the importance of strong communication and partnership working between fragmented provision as well as with parents

- consider our own attitudes towards 'school readiness' and how we ensure that our practice is developmentally appropriate

- engage policy-makers, senior leaders, head teachers and managers etc. in the transitions debate, challenge them to consider organisational change where possible, and to be proactive in finding practical solutions to the daily challenges of transition faced by some children.

4

Reflecting on our own experience of transition

This chapter will look more closely at our own experiences of change and transition and how these can help us empathise with the children and families we work with. Putting oneself 'in the shoes of the child' is not just a useful exercise – it is also a vital part of our professional responsibility as reflective practitioners. This chapter will also refer to some of the major theorists who have researched and written about children's transitions and explore how their work can help us to better understand the experience from a child's point of view. Scenarios of a range of children in different settings provide a context for further reflection.

REFLECTION TASK

Have a think about . . . your own attitudes to change.

■ Think back to a time when you were starting a new job. Make a list of the feelings you associate with that time.
■ Here are a few – you will have more.

anticipation	enthusiasm	fear of making
hopefulness	challenge	mistakes
fear of the unknown	uncertainty	lack of control over
stressed	bewilderment	situation
excitement	nervousness	self-doubt
anxiety		

Mixed emotions about change

We consider it normal to have mixed feelings when starting a new job. Even if we are enthusiastic and excited about the new challenge before us, we would expect to have a degree of nervousness as we face the unfamiliar. Even in situations where change is less dramatic, e.g. taking on a new position within the same establishment, there are still likely to be different expectations of us, even if the environment remains the same. This might perhaps be in the way we are expected to work, or the degrees of responsibility we need to assume. In a brand new job that has come about as a result of an unwanted circumstance or change, the stressful feelings might possibly outweigh any potential enthusiasm or hopefulness.

As an adult in this situation, we do at least know what is happening to us. We understand that we are undergoing change, even if we aren't happy about it. Elinor Goldschmied and Sonia Jackson pointed out something we should never forget when we think about children undergoing their earliest transitions from home:

> We can never remind ourselves too often that a child, particularly a very young and almost totally dependent one, is the only person in the nursery who cannot understand why he is there. He can only explain it as abandonment, and unless he is helped in a positive and affectionate way, this will mean levels of anxiety greater than he can tolerate.
>
> (Goldschmied and Jackson 1994:37)

How empathy supports our practice

If we try to put ourselves 'in the shoes' of the children we work with, then it is good to reflect on the mix of feelings and emotions associated with change and transition. In the first instance, we can perhaps relate to the children we ourselves once were and connect with our own feelings about the transitions that we had to go through in our early lives. Reading the previous chapter might have triggered memories and feelings for you about being cared for outside your home or starting nursery or school.

- Do you remember feeling anxious and uncertain?
- Did you worry that you might be abandoned – that no-one would come back for you?
- Or perhaps you were excited and curious?
- How much did you understand about what was happening?
- How much control did you feel you had?

The baby being left with a childminder or daycare provider cannot possibly know or understand why they are there, even if the parent or practitioner tries to explain.

The words 'Mummy's going to work now, she'll be back soon' will come to mean something eventually, but certainly not in the first instance.

The young child moving from room to room within a setting, or from nursery class to reception in the same primary school, might recognise the familiar environment but will be experiencing different expectations of them 'now they are bigger'. A child who is changing settings or moving schools will have had no control in the decision to move and may well not understand the reason for it.

Knowing a bit more about attachment theory can perhaps help us to make sense of the ways in which we responded to change in our early life – and also lead to an appreciation of how we cope with transition now as adults. For some people, change of any kind will always be stressful and they will try to avoid it at all costs. There are others who seem to seek out change as if they are constantly searching for something. There are some who have a healthy attitude to change – seeking it only when appropriate and able to thrive in response.

Can you see any links between your answers to the reflection task and your own early experiences of change and transition? How does this make you feel? Drawing on these feelings can help us understand and empathise with the children and families we work with, but, as was stated in Chapter 1, please make sure you seek help and advice if thinking about these things makes you feel particularly uncomfortable or distressed.

Supportive environments: what helps us through transition

As well as our own inner resources and dispositions towards change, there are positive situations and environments that can help us handle change and transition.

REFLECTION TASK

Have a think about ... your experiences of changing or starting a new job.

■ What has made a positive difference to that experience?
■ If you have had negative experiences, what do you think would have helped improve the experience?

Opportunities to familiarise yourself?	Feeling safe enough to take risks?	Being warmly welcomed?
Being eagerly awaited?	Realistic expectations of you?	Some predictability in routines?
Treated with respect?		
Having time to settle in?	Having a 'buddy' – someone to show you the ropes?	Feeling like a fish in water?
Allowed some control?		
Feeling valued?		
Feeling you belonged?	Being with a friend?	

A fish in water

Having some or all of these things in place can make a big difference to how quickly we settle into a new job and begin to feel like 'a fish in water'. What does this mean exactly? It's more usual to think of the parallel phrase, 'a fish out of water' – the usual definition of which is someone who feels unsuited to where they are. So a 'fish in water' is the opposite – someone who is exactly where they are supposed to be – who feels suited to the situation in which they find themselves.

This concept features in a lot of writing about early years transitions. Aline-Wendy Dunlop quotes the French sociologist, Bourdieu, who writes that when a fish is in water 'it does not feel the weight of the water and it takes the world about itself for granted' (Dunlop and Fabian 2007:159, citing Bourdieu and Waquant 1992). In the English translation of the manual edited by Ferre Laevers (for assessing well being and involvement in care settings) it is described very simply. 'Like a fish in water' – that is how you can describe children who feel 'alright' (Laevers 2005:7). Feeling 'alright' might not be a very technical term, but it is a term we can all relate to. Stig Brostrom, writing in *Transitions in the Early Years*, edited by Dunlop and Fabian (2002:52), talks of 'feeling suitable' and describes this as 'crucial to the child's learning and development as well as to a fundamental and continuous sense of well-being'.

A fish feels suitable in water because it has enough of what it needs – and once it's there it doesn't really need to think much about its environment – it just is right. A fish out of water, though, doesn't just feel odd – the conditions are not suitable for its survival, so it cannot thrive and although it energetically resists and 'fights' the new environment, it ultimately will not survive. Sounds extreme – but this can happen to some children in educational contexts. They don't thrive, they use up valuable energy in resistance, and their motivation for learning doesn't survive the experience.

Belonging

A fish 'belongs' in water – and the concept of belonging is very important when we think about the development of emotional health. In New Zealand, 'belonging' forms one of the strands of *Te Whāriki*, the Ministry of Education's early childhood curriculum policy statement. 'The early childhood education setting should be like a caring home: a secure and safe place where each member is entitled to respect and to the best of care. The feeling of belonging, in the widest sense, contributes to inner well-being, security, and identity' (www.educate.ece.govt.nz/learning/curriculumAndLearning/TeWhariki/PartC/StrandsandGoals/StrandTwoBelonging.aspx).

As adults, settling into a new place of work or moving to a new area we know the subtle signs that tell us we do – or don't yet – belong in our new environment. Often a sense of 'culture shock' accompanies a sense of not belonging. In the work context, perhaps the ways of working are very different to what we're used to.

Moving to a new town, we might find people talking with a different accent or using words we're not used to for familiar things. In a different country the culture shock can be even greater, even if language is not a consideration as we deal with different foods and customs, as well as unfamiliar bureaucratic and administration systems. Sociologists and educationalists recognise that children often experience a similar culture shock when they are cared for outside of their home. This is particularly the case for children from minority ethnic and linguistic communities, but can be just as relevant for children from all communities. Playgroup, nursery, reception class can all be culturally worlds away from a child's home experience, in ways that are not always obvious.

Bourdieu's theory of habitus and transitions

Bourdieu linked his appreciation of how it feels to be a fish in water with the concept he called *habitus*. Liz Brooker describes this as 'a set of dispositions towards life which informs what people say and do (and how they bring up their children). The *habitus* is shaped by any family's history, and geography, their social class and ethnicity, their experiences of education and employment, work and travel and their social networks' (Brooker 2008:62).

Each will be subtly different but will have some features in common, if not with *every* other family, at least with others who share for example, a local community, a language, a religion, a socioeconomic group or other identifying feature. Liz Brooker suggests that 'every family has its own unique home culture, which shares some characteristics with similar families but is the product of beliefs and values which the family members have acquired through their own life experiences' (Brooker 2008:56).

And it's not just the routines and rituals of family life that make up a child's familiar experience. It's also the family's expectations, their world view and the way that each individual child within a family absorbs these. If a child's *habitus* fits more or less with the social world of the nursery or school that they are moving into, then there is less of a culture shock. A child whose *habitus* does not fit so well is more likely to feel like a 'fish out of water'.

Bourdieu also explored the concept of 'cultural capital' – the idea that some aspects of a child's home culture are worth more than others in the context of educational environments. In an article for *NALDIC News*, A. Blackledge comments on how schools use ways of talking, patterns of discipline and models for learning that will be unfamiliar to some children, while others will start school or nursery already comfortable with them, because they more closely match their experiences at home.

> Bourdieu argues that while the cultural capital that is valued in schools is not equally available to children from different backgrounds, schools still operate as if all students had equal access to it. That is, those students whose familial socialisation endows them with the kind of cultural capital that is similar to

that of the school are likely to do well in their schooling; those students whose familial socialisation gives them a cultural capital which is remote from that of the school are less likely to do well.

(Blackledge 2000)

This acknowledges that there may be much in a child's home culture that is valuable – it's just not valued and credited within a school context. Sadly this isn't exclusively a 'school' issue. Some children and their parents may experience similar culture shocks when joining a voluntary playgroup or registering for daycare, and this obviously can have a big impact on their adjustment as they attempt to settle in.

For this reason, I have always found it more relevant to refer to a young child's experience level rather than level of ability. A child arriving in a school or pre-school setting with a wealth of positive literacy experiences (e.g. supportive exposure to books, stories and rhymes written and told in English) is more likely to be assessed as 'able' with regard to pre-literacy skills, simply because they already have a good working knowledge of books and print conventions in English, even if they are not actively reading yet. A child who, for whatever reason, does not have that experience, may find themselves described as less able, long before any real 'ability' can be formally assessed.

Language in particular is an important factor in *habitus*, and as Brooker comments,

We know too, from decades of research, that the kinds of language children hear and acquire in their homes are not all equally valued in their classrooms (Bernstein 1971; Heath 1983; Michaels 1986). Not only bilingual children, but many monolingual English speaking children, acquire their earliest knowledge and skills by means of a language which is significantly different from the language of teachers, and which does not serve them well when they make the transition to school (Tizard and Hughes 1984; Wells 1985).

(Brooker 2008:64)

Supportive environments make a difference to transition

Take another look at the suggestions in the reflection task on p. 53 and those you thought of for yourself. What might each of those look like in the real life of a child who is making that first transition to a care setting outside their home? And just as importantly, what is the experience like for their parents?

Let's take some of them and make them real.

Being eagerly awaited

Freddie is starting school. His reception class teacher Alva has visited him at home and at his pre-school group. She brought with her Jo, who is the teaching assistant in the class and will be a key person for Freddie.

Freddie and his mum, Karla, are met at the door by Alva. She smiles with genuine warmth and pleasure at their arrival. She tells them how much she and Jo have been looking forward to seeing them again and how pleased they are that Freddie has come to join them in class 1. She tells them that Jo is playing inside with the sand and waiting for Freddie. He runs in eagerly and Alva spends a few minutes checking in with Karla, reassuring her she can stay as long as she likes.

Karla visibly relaxes and settles herself in a corner where she can watch Freddie as he plays with Jo for a while. Alva and Karla agree that Freddie seems fine, and Alva invites Karla to go and have a coffee in the parents' room, reassuring her that they will call her if Freddie becomes anxious.

A warm welcome

Tanika and her mum, Joy, arrive at the childminder's house for her first full day after a two week settling process. Beverley meets them at the gate with a smile and an encouraging word for mum, who is anxious about her return to work. She brings them both into the house and settles them on the sofa, where she has some familiar toys waiting for Tanika. She acknowledges how Joy must be feeling and talks reassuringly with her until she is ready to leave for work. Although still anxious, Joy feels confident that her toddler will be well looked after by Beverley.

Treated with respect

David's family have had to move house halfway through his reception year, and he will be changing schools. They are visiting the new school for the first time. They arrive early for their appointment at 9.30 and the head teacher is still busy meeting parents and children at the school entrance. She greets everyone by name and chats with them as they enter the building. She notices David and his dad and introduces them to the school secretary and to a parent helper who will be working with David's class. She shows them to the waiting area and says she will be with them shortly when she has 'settled the school in for the day'.

David and his dad look at the displays and photos on the wall and read the scrapbooks made by the children of last term's projects and outings. At 9.30 the head teacher comes to collect them to show them round the school, apologising for their wait and thanking them for their patience. David's dad is pleasantly surprised by the care and consideration shown to them, and feels reassured that David will be OK in his new school.

Time to settle in

Mary has been in nursery school for three weeks. She doesn't cry or show distress when mum leaves, but looks a little sad and is reluctant to join in with activities either with children or adults. The only activity she has shown any real interest in, so far, has been the box of big wooden beads and threading laces. This has been on a table that has a good vantage point for viewing the room and the one adjoining it through an open archway.

Staff have noticed that Mary likes to sit and watch what is going on in both rooms while she threads the beads. They agreed to make sure this activity continues to be available at this table for as long as Mary seems to need it, and that careful observation will help them to monitor her well-being. They haven't rushed her to join in with other activities and have noticed her become increasingly relaxed and beginning to make eye contact and responsive gestures to other children.

Mum has been reassured that Mary is being carefully supported to settle in and tells staff that she talks animatedly at home in her first language about nursery and all the activities she has observed children and staff engaging with. She wakes up early at the weekends wanting to come to nursery!

Feeling safe enough to take risks

Anjuli has been to the pre-school several times with her mum Ronita. Anjuli has ventured outside on her own for the first time today. Mum sits by the blockplay area just inside the door, where she can see Anjuli and where Anjuli can just see her. At first, Anjuli comes inside every few minutes and leans against Ronita's knee or climbs in her lap. Within a minute or two she is off out again. After a while she feels safe enough to branch out to the far side of the garden and stay away a bit longer.

Mum nips to the loo and asks the practitioner, Betty, to watch out for Anjuli coming in and looking for her. Betty spots Anjuli on her way in and reassures her that mum will be back in a minute or two. She engages her in conversation about the toy she has brought in from outside, until mum returns.

Ronita has watched and celebrated Anjuli's growing confidence in playing away from her and was reassured by Betty's attention to both their needs. She knew she could trust that her child's need for security was understood and that for herself, it was safe enough to take the huge risk of leaving her precious child in the care of the pre-school practitioners.

Allowed some control

Carl has been coming to nursery for a few weeks. His key person Rick is tuning into his need for energetic activity and has observed that his fine motor control is excellent. He can sustain concentration really well when occupied with small world and construction toys, and is happiest outdoors where he has lots of room for running, jumping, climbing, etc.

Rick is introducing Carl to small group times gradually, and not insisting that he joins them unless he seems keen. When he does, the focus is on storytelling with props and singing finger rhymes and action songs. Carl is given lots of opportunity to lead and make choices about the songs they sing. Mum is pleased with the way Carl is settling and happily reports that Carl has told her he 'loves' Rick.

Realistic expectations

Mack seems to be coping with school OK. He had attended the school's nursery class and was familiar with the reception class from when his older brother had been in the same class a year earlier. Three weeks into the new term the teacher takes the children into the school hall for their first experience of a PE session. Mack refuses to take off his clothes and put on his PE kit. He has played on the equipment in the hall before, but is really unhappy about removing and changing his clothes. The teacher recognises Mack's distress and allows him to sit with a practitioner he knows well who after a while is able to persuade him to remove his socks and shoes. He then spends a few minutes using the apparatus until the end of the session.

Over the rest of the term, Mack is supported by the practitioner to begin to remove only what he feels comfortable with and allowed to explore the equipment safely at his own pace. After the Christmas holiday, Mack comes to school happily bearing his PE bag and changes for PE with no problems. Mum and dad were asked if there might be any underlying reason why Mack is unhappy about changing for PE, but were reassured by the school that this wasn't unusual and that there was no expectation that they should pressure him in any way.

His parents were relieved that Mack wasn't being judged as awkward or tiresome and that he wouldn't miss out on the PE session because of his anxiety. They appreciated the support and the caring attitude and acknowledged that the teacher's gentle approach was more likely to be successful than if they rushed or penalised him.

Having a buddy . . . Being with a friend

Hardeep, Jake and Sonny have been friends since their mums were pregnant together. They are all starting soon at the three-form reception unit of their local primary school. They are scheduled to be in separate classes, but at the home visits their parents point out how supportive their friendship has been and their concerns when they hear they will be split up. The staff explain that they will still see each other outdoors and other shared parts of the day, but on reflection they agree that the friendship could play an important part in supporting their transition and place the boys together in the same group. They assure the parents that the boys will have plenty of opportunities to build their own identities even when they are together, and that the situation will be regularly reviewed. The option to change groupings should it become more appropriate could occur when the boys were older and well settled at school.

The parents were happy with the response to their concerns – they felt the school's openness to their input and its flexible approach was encouraging and appropriate. Just as importantly, they were also reassured that the boys' needs as individuals would be addressed and that the situation would be regularly reviewed to ensure it was still in all their best interests.

Feeling valued

Kyle's mum, Leanne, was very nervous about the home visit from the nursery. Kyle wasn't fully toilet trained and she thought they might tell her he couldn't start yet. The practitioners Hasina and Marjorie who came to visit reassured her that wasn't a problem and as they talked and played with Kyle, Leanne began to relax a bit. She told them how much she wanted Kyle to do well in school, but she was worried that he might turn out to have learning difficulties.

As Kyle took Marjorie off to show her his bedroom, Leanne confided to Hasina that she had hated school, and had been permanently excluded for assaulting a teacher. Hasina reassured Leanne that Kyle would be settling in gradually to nursery and that mum could stay as long as she liked with him. She also suggested that once he was settled, Leanne might like to join their parent volunteer group and help out if she had the time. Leanne laughed and said she'd be no good doing reading and writing, but Hasina pointed out that there would be lots of things she could do including cooking. Leanne agreed she'd like that – she used to be good at baking cakes. After the visit Marjorie and Hasina discussed possible lines of support for Leanne, as well as continued encouragement to get involved in volunteer activities at the nursery.

Some predictability in routines

Jordie has been at school for a term and a half. He and his mum are now very familiar with the daily routine of arrival and self-registration. He always likes to hang up his coat and find his name card by himself, but needs mum to help him with his zip and put his hat and gloves in his tray.

He says goodbye to mum and then heads straight for the garage and cars, which are always available over by the block corner. Mum knows that the routine seems to 'settle' Jordie and that the rest of his day involves lots of opportunities for trying new activities at his own pace.

It's the little things that make a difference . . .

These positive experiences are not just making the current transition easier or smoother – they are also building a firm foundation of emotional health and well-being that has longer term implications for the future. There are positive connections being made in the brains of these children, which are also awash with 'feel-good' chemicals. The reassurance and security that these experiences provide are building a sense of safety, security and 'being cared for' in the children (as well as their parents) which has longer term implications. They create a safety net of emotional health that's 'good enough' to hold them in good stead later, when circumstances may be less advantageous.

How do these positive experiences build resilience for other less positive times?

Positive experience builds resilience of a healthy kind. There are strong similarities between these kinds of experiences and the cycle of regulation that was described in Chapter 1. Having enough repeated evidence that we are cared for and 'cared about' helps to build our trust in others – and our confidence in ourselves. This means a higher likelihood not only that we can view the next experience of change with more confidence and resilience, but that our brains will also allow us to embrace the positive aspects of transition with enthusiasm and hopefulness.

But what if our experiences of transition are not so positive?

Here are the same children but in less supportive circumstances.

Freddie and the other 29 children in his reception class are starting full-time school. He has had a week of half days and his mum was invited to a meeting to hear about what will be required of her once he has begun school. She was told about the uniform and behaviour policy, the literacy and numeracy programme and how much school dinners cost and the procedure for paying for them. Parents were informed that when full-time school started they would need to leave their children at the school gate in time for the bell when they would be required to line up in their class group. The teaching assistant collected the children from the playground on the first day and held Freddie's hand as she could see that he was tearful. She waved at mum and told her not to worry.

Tanika and Joy arrive at the childminder's house. They ring the bell and wait a few minutes before ringing again. Beverley's husband answers the door on his way out and tells them to go through. Beverley tells Joy she'll be with her in a minute; she is just on the phone and won't be long. Joy is anxious as it's her first proper day back at work and Tanika starts to fuss and become agitated. Beverley finishes her call and takes her from mum as Tanika begins to shriek. She ushers mum to the door, telling her she'll give her a ring later if there are any problems.

David and his dad arrive early for their 9.30 appointment and are told to wait outside the office. A number of parents are also waiting by the head's office hoping to get to see her this morning. The school secretary suggests to those waiting that they make an appointment and reminds them of the school's 'open door policy' between 2–3 pm Tuesdays and Thursdays. The head teacher sees but doesn't acknowledge David and his dad as she pops in and out of her office talking to staff and answering the phone. At 9.40, the secretary tells them the head is dealing with an important matter and will be with them shortly. Dad tries to occupy David by playing 'I spy' until they are finally shown into the office just after 10.00am.

Mary looked for the beads when she came in. They weren't on the usual table as staff had a policy of rotating manipulative activities every two days. It was peg boards today. She sat at the table anyway for a while until her key worker told her to come and sit on the carpet for group time. She came and sat down with the others but didn't join in with the song or want to hold the shell when it was her turn. She couldn't find the beads again the next day but seemed to like making the pasta necklace when it was her turn to go to the 'making' table.

By the time the beads were available again the following week, Mary was off with a temperature. When she returned to nursery she was weepy and unsettled. Her mum said she cried every morning and she was worried about her. Staff assured mum that they all settle down eventually. Mary's attendance continued to be a cause for concern throughout her time at the nursery and staff were able to give very little information about her to the reception teacher when the time came to transfer to school, although they suggested she might have language delay and learning needs.

Anjuli's mum, Ronita, asked the practitioner (she wasn't sure of her name) if she would watch out for Anjuli while she quickly went to the loo. The practitioner said 'yes , no problem, but am sure she'll be fine – it's not like you've gone far!' She watched for Anjuli for a minute or two and then was distracted by two boys arguing in the far corner. Anjuli came in and couldn't see her mum. She ran to the door and shouted for her mummy. When Ronita came in by another door, Anjuli ran to her and burst into tears. Ronita felt terrible at having left her, and Anjuli wouldn't leave her side for the rest of the session.

Carl finds it hard to sit still at carpet time. He calls out and jumps up and down. The practitioner tells him to come and sit next to her on the floor. He finds a small world figure under the chair and fiddles with it. The practitioner takes it away from him. He shouts out during the story and fiddles with the Velcro fasteners on his shoes. This makes a loud noise and the practitioner takes off his shoes. He kicks his legs out and proceeds to take off his socks. The practitioner calls for the parent helper in the class to take him out of the room and sit with him till the story is finished.

Mack refuses to get changed for PE. He is brought to the hall with the other children and told to sit on the bench and watch. A practitioner later tries to take off his shoes and socks but he kicks her. His parents are informed that there has been a problem but that they will not enforce school behaviour policy on this occasion as they are sure he didn't really mean to kick Mrs B, but would they please practise putting on his PE kit at home. Health and safety policy means he can't do PE unless he is wearing the school kit, and he will have to sit out if he won't get changed.

Hardeep, Jake and Sonny are all in different classes in the three-form reception unit at their primary school. Hardeep and Sonny seem to be coping OK, although neither seems enthusiastic about going to school after the initial excitement has worn off. Jake, however, is finding it very hard to settle and his mother approaches his class teacher and asks if he might be able to spend time playing with either of his friends from home. The teacher points out that they see each other at playtime every day anyway and that there have been some incidents of 'boisterous play' when the three of them got together. In her opinion they are better off apart as they seem to 'set each other off'. She reassures mum that 'They'll make new friends and widen their horizons if they don't have each other to rely on'.

Kyle's mum is informed by the nursery that they won't be able to admit him until he is fully toilet trained. Leanne has no further contact with the nursery, and by the time Kyle is school age he has been taken into care and mum is in a psychiatric hospital.

Jordie has been in school for a while now but he and his mum both still find the transition difficult at the start of the school day. Some days the children are allowed to play with activities for a while before coming to the carpet for registration. Other days they have to go straight to the carpet as they need to be up in the hall for assembly by 9.10. Mum never knows for certain what is happening that morning, as it seems to change a lot. Jordie often 'plays up' on the way to school and mum feels very stressed when she gets there, particularly if the teacher and other children are all waiting for them on the carpet. Some days Jordie refuses to take his coat off in the cloakroom and has a temper tantrum.

Flexible approach

None of these negative scenarios are about adults deliberately being difficult or uncaring. Very often they are carrying out policies and day-to-day routines that have built up over time and been considered good – or at least acceptable – practice.

They are arrived at because of convention or convenience and some sense of how transitions (and the children and families experiencing them) need to be 'managed' in order to cause least disruption. The 'one size fits all' approach to transition doesn't allow for the needs of the individual child and their family. But the examples in the first set of scenarios show us just what a difference flexibility and personal attention can make to the individual, without being overly disruptive to the setting. Transition policies that have such flexibility and care for the needs of the individual designed into them are likely to be the most effective and successful.

They also make for a better working environment. Have another quick look at the positive scenarios and register how they make you feel. It's possible that just by reading them you are getting a burst of feel-good chemicals in the brain, so how much more enjoyable to be part of that experience and know that your input as a practitioner, childminder or head teacher has had such a positive effect on the life of a child and their family? An environment that is genuinely welcoming and caring will demonstrate a willingness to respond to the needs of the individual. This is more likely to generate relaxed children and families, which, as well as making work less stressful for the staff, reassures them that the same degree of care and respect is likely to be shown to their own needs and emotional well-being.

Impact on learning

We considered the impact of stress chemicals on a baby's developing brain in Chapter 2. If we look again at the negative experiences in the second set of scenarios, we can see evidence of stress for the children and families involved – and possibly also the people who work with them.

We know that a brain flooded with cortisol is not fully functioning. So what can we assume about the level of learning accessed by Mary, Mack, Carl and the others in the situations outlined on pp. 64–5? Poor Kyle doesn't even get the chance to make the transition to nursery – and with far-reaching consequences. We know that we want 'smooth transitions' for children so that learning is not disrupted, but are we always able to recognise how 'bumpy' these transitions actually are for some of our children – and how this is reflected in their learning and acknowledged in our assessments of their 'ability levels'?

The importance of getting off to a good start

The children who are best able to make a flying start or to 'hit the ground running', and make the most of the learning opportunities at each transition, are those whose early experiences have been consistently positive and whose previous experience of change has been well supported. Each transition that is handled thoughtfully and appropriately for a child builds resilience and positivity for the next change that might come along. A negative experience not only delays the learning that can take place at that time; it seems also to increase the likelihood of interrupted learning the next time the child has to endure a transition.

TABLE 1 Survival strategies and behaviours

SURVIVAL STRATEGIES	BEHAVIOURS
Shutting down emotions	Withdrawn; extreme reserve and shyness; glazing over; blanking out
Frequent use of self-soothing/self-harm behaviours	Thumb sucking; nail biting; skin picking; rocking; head banging
Avoiding situations that have negative associations	Running away; refusing to join in; delaying tactics
Being overly compliant	Over-eager to please; unassertive; showing no independence or initiative
Being excessively clingy	Sticking close to someone else; highly selective of who they engage with; overpowering/monopolising of a friend; fearful of separations
Attention seeking	Negative behaviours; asking for constant reassurance; heightened sensitivity; overreaction to small hurts

Rather than the healthy resilience that comes with early positive experiences, negative experiences that take place too soon and too often are more likely to create survival strategies and behaviours. These are much less healthy. Think back to the regulation cycle in Chapter 1 and the possible short and longer term impact on the brain of a lack of positive response.

Table 1 gives some of the sort of survival strategies and accompanying behaviours that any of us might use in difficult or extreme circumstances. These strategies help us to cope in the moment but are not likely to be helpful in the long run. Positive experiences are about so much more than just 'coping'. Lots of energy, whether physical or emotional, will be required to keep going through the negative experience – energy that is being used up and is therefore not available for other physical or mental activity. Similarly, the stress chemicals flooding some parts of the brain mean they become unavailable for thinking.

Coping more or less means we are in 'survival' mode. This is fine if it is momentary or in times of real crisis, but if it is ongoing and part of 'normal' experience it is not allowing other healthy brain-building activity to take place and it is also raising the level of stress chemicals that the brain is regularly exposed to. As Richard Bowlby reminds us:

> The chronic stress of repeated separations can show as subtle behaviour and mood changes, but these are easily misunderstood and are often interpreted as babies and toddlers settling in and accepting their new surroundings. However their saliva cortisol levels are elevated, and their behaviour is often not the same as it is when they're at home.
>
> (R. Bowlby 2007)

REFLECTION TASK

Have a think about . . . what it was like learning to drive. Stressful? Confusing? Tiring?

If you have successfully learned to drive, then it has probably now become an everyday, automatic experience for you, that you take in your stride. A high degree of alertness is required, but your mastery and confidence is such that you can concentrate on the manoeuvres involved in driving the car, negotiation of the road and other drivers and memory of the Highway Code – while at the same time holding a conversation, following route directions, planning tonight's dinner or singing along to the radio. But this probably wasn't the case in the early stages of learning, when there may have been a degree of stress even for the most confident. The process was probably also quite tiring. Most stressful of all was probably the day you took your driving test.

Have another think about . . .
If driving every day involved the same degree of stress as you experienced doing your test, do you think you would choose to keep doing it?

- What if you had no choice and you had to keep doing it but with the same level of fear or stress?
- What would be the effect on your ability and skills level?
- What needs to happen to allow car drivers to maintain a healthy 'alertness' but be comfortable enough to be willing to do it regularly and be relaxed enough to do it safely?

We have to assume that for most people, confidence as a driver is strongly linked with their growing physical mastery – which is reinforced by regular, repeated positive experiences of driving, alongside a minimum of negative experiences, e.g. failed manoeuvres, accidents and near misses. If the experience every time you get in the car is fraught with difficulties and close shaves – or, just as importantly, the FEAR of them – you are likely to be always driving with a high level of stress, which in turn isn't conducive to skilful driving.

The child for whom being away from home is still stressful, despite appearing to 'cope', is possibly having to function in a high stress level all the time. What might that look like?

- lack of attention
- poor concentration
- poor attitude or motivation

- lack of self-control
- behaviour difficulties
- poor social skills
- poor self-help (low levels of self-resilience)
- unwillingness to be taught (extreme self-resilience)
- anxiety
- needing lots of reassurance
- poor initiative.

These are some aspects that might be evident in the setting and may (or may not) be identified as having learning implications.

Or the child may not cause concern in the setting, but their anxiety is played out at home where the child feels 'safe enough' to let go. So the family might experience bedwetting, poor sleeping, anxiety about going to school, or challenging/unusual behaviour at home that doesn't appear to be linked to the transition, particularly if it took place some time ago.

Or maybe none of these – the child has a high level of coping skills and appears to be doing OK, but actually is never capable of reaching their true potential because their stress levels are always high and they simply never feel relaxed enough.

A window of stress tolerance

Everyone has a window of stress tolerance – just how much input from external situations you can cope with before becoming overwhelmed by the stress chemicals flooding the brain. This window is kept healthy and wide open when there are (or have been) enough positive experiences to balance out the negative. Without enough of the 'feel-good stuff' in the first place (the kinds of 'good enough' experiences that build resilience) the window is already almost closed – so it doesn't take much to slam it shut. We see this in adults every day in examples of 'road rage', when small incidents can result in huge overreactions. Children have stress tolerance levels too, and for some, it really doesn't take very much to tip them over the edge. Sadly, adults don't always recognise this and make sweeping judgements about children's behaviour that don't take account of the levels of resilience a child may have, or the impact of stress on their reactions to daily experiences.

'Honeymoon period'

What does all this have to tell us about the so-called 'honeymoon period'?

We tend to hear this phrase being used when a child appears to be 'doing fine' for several weeks and then suddenly, for no obvious reason, starts to display behaviours that suggest separation anxiety etc. We tend to attribute this to the child realising that going to school is now 'for ever', i.e. it's not just an interesting, short-lived experience. But it might be that the child, in reality, was stressed by the 'coping experience' and so did not have a healthy window of stress tolerance. This window has now just been slammed shut by a trigger (maybe tiny but highly relevant to the child) that remains unrecognised by the child's family and the practitioners working with them.

Goldschmied and Jackson remind us how, for a small child, separation can feel like a bereavement and the process of grieving often includes a delayed reaction. 'Adults who have lost someone they love often report unexpected bursts of misery long after they had thought they had come to terms with their loss' (Goldschmied and Jackson 1994:47). Children too can suddenly be overwhelmed by misery in the midst of seeming to be happy and comfortable, long after the initial settling period.

We can address this by careful monitoring and watchfulness, but also by refusing to treat transition as something that is over and done within a few weeks. If we are more aware of the process, we are much less likely to be surprised by the reactions of our children. Even more importantly, we can work hard to reduce the possible stress triggers, as well as honouring and acknowledging those that may inevitably occur. It is not fair to tell a child missing their parent that they don't 'need' to cry or be sad. Better to acknowledge how they really feel and show them we understand and are there to help them with those feelings – not to deny them. 'Distress needs to be expressed in a context of quiet acceptance, in the same way that we would try to comfort an adult experiencing loss and grief' (Goldschmied and Jackson 1994:47). Big boys and girls certainly do need to cry, along with little ones of all ages.

Building resilience through positive experiences

From what we've seen so far, then, attachment theory suggests (and neuroscience would seem to confirm) that the popular adage that 'what doesn't kill you, makes you stronger' isn't strictly true, and that wherever possible we should aim for young children to have lots of positive experiences. But even in ideal circumstances we cannot protect children from every one of the negative experiences they are likely to have to deal with in the real world. However, we mustn't forget that as practitioners, it is our responsibility to compensate where we can for the less than ideal circumstances experienced by some children. Just as importantly, we must absolutely make sure that our actions (or lack of them) don't create or contribute to any further unnecessary damaging or negative experiences.

Maria Robinson writes:

Several researchers point out that while experience is important for healthy development in all areas, additional enrichment of the child's environment beyond what is 'normal' for most children seems to have little effect. The

picture that seems to be emerging is that it is impoverished environments –
whether emotional, cognitive, social or physical, that appear to make the
difference, not enriched ones.

(Robinson 2003:20)

Let's think again about the scenarios in the earlier part of this chapter

Here is another layer of information to add to what you already know about the
children and their families.

Freddie was recently placed for adoption. He has been with his new family for
three months. He survived serious neglect in his birth family and experienced
several changes of foster carer before being adopted.

Tanika is recovering from a severe ear infection and may have a hearing
impairment. Joy is a single parent, returning to work as a maths teacher after taking
extended maternity leave.

David and his dad have moved to a new area following mum's imprisonment for
manslaughter due to dangerous driving.

Mary is from a family of refugees. Her father was killed shortly before they fled
their home country. Her mother speaks three languages fluently, including English.
Mary understands English quite well, although she is not using it yet with
confidence.

Anjuli was born 12 weeks prematurely and weighed 2 lbs. She was not expected
to survive and has had several extended hospital stays. She walked at 18 months
but was slow to begin speaking. She is making good physical progress now,
although her eyesight and speech delay are being monitored.

Carl is learning English as an additional language. He speaks Polish at home.

Mack is the youngest of four boys. His birth was complicated and he was delivered
by emergency C-section. He finds it hard to tolerate some sensations, and rages
easily when touched. He will be diagnosed with a sensory integration disorder
when he is six years old, which will be dramatically improved with neurodevelop-
mental reorganisation therapy.

Jake has Down's Syndrome. His health is very good and with support from a home
visiting Portage worker before starting school he has made excellent progress and
met most of his developmental milestones.

Kyle was born to a teenage mother with undiagnosed mental health difficulties, who has recently left the care system.

Jordie is on the autistic spectrum.

Now read both sets of scenarios again, bearing this new information in mind.

Entitlement to care and respect

The 'positive' scenarios remain positive, regardless of whether or not the children in question have special needs or their families are in crisis.

Freddie is entitled to feel eagerly awaited whether or not his home life to date has been one of complete safety and nurture. Tanika's mum needs to feel warmth in the welcome she receives from the woman with whom she is leaving her child, and David and his dad deserve respectful attention on their first visit to a new school, regardless of their home circumstances.

Professionals who take their responsibilities seriously are a must for Mary, Anjuli, Carl and Mack – they benefit from practitioners who are skilled in relationships and interactions and who know that observations and attunement are the key to 'meeting children where they are at' and moving them forward, regardless of their starting point or particular circumstances. Kyle and his mother both need support from astute professionals who will take the time to understand their needs and value their contributions, while keeping a close professional eye on them. Jake and Jordie need educational systems that are consistent, but flexible enough to adapt to their needs so they can achieve their potential with – or without – a diagnosis of special educational need.

Vulnerable children and families

But what of the 'negative' scenarios? We've already explored some of the effects that 'bumpy' transition experiences can have on young children. Let's go even deeper and consider the potential impact on our children and families who are most vulnerable, and particularly so at times of change.

Tearful Freddie being whisked into school with his mum waving at the gate is a hard enough scenario to bear for any of us – but how much harder if both mum and child are still learning to attach to each other? Can you imagine the terror for Freddie, who has seen several 'mums' come and go in his short life, some of them never to be seen again? How can he know that he will ever see this mum again?

Choosing a childminder and returning to work is a difficult thing for anyone to do, but imagine Joy's feelings on that first morning, knowing that Beverley isn't prepared to welcome them with the calm and soothing approach that both of them need on such a difficult day.

Waiting outside a head teacher's office can be anxiety-inducing for many of us – even at the best of times. David and his dad have already experienced a lot of shock and trauma over the last year since the car accident, mum's imprisonment and their enforced move as a result of hostility in their old neighbourhood. The last thing they need is to be treated with indifference, as dad's anxious state of mind interprets this as yet more hostility. The warmth and respect shown by the head teacher in the first scenario is nothing more than it should be – this is an entitlement of each and every visitor to the school. But how much more of a powerful impact does it have in this situation where it signals the likelihood that this child's transition will improve the quality of his life, rather than damage it further?

Mary and her mother have already experienced trauma and dramatic change to their lives. Mary is right to be watchful and vigilant about what is going on around her, to take time to become accustomed to new experiences. She chooses activities that soothe and help keep her calm while she goes through 'the silent' or 'studial' period of developing an additional language – waiting until she feels confident in her ability before speaking out in English. In the supportive environment of the first scenario, there is reassuring evidence of gradual progress, backed up by the information from home. The second scenario fails Mary and her parent in just about every way imaginable.

Mack's special needs are not yet diagnosed although his parents are anxious that something isn't quite right. The inclusive and flexible approach in the first scenario allows Mack to build confidence gradually and alerts practitioners to the kinds of support he will require, while they continue to monitor him carefully. Working in partnership with his parents will mean that a diagnosis is reached sooner rather than later and with little damage to his confidence and self-image. The rigidity of the second scenario leaves little scope for practitioners to recognise conditions that are less well known and creates an environment in which Mack has little chance of thriving.

Ronita has every reason to be anxious about Anjuli's physical and emotional well-being. The trauma for parents of children born very prematurely doesn't end when they finally get to bring their baby home. As more babies survive increasingly premature birth, we are slowly becoming more aware of the possible effects on their emotional and cognitive development as well as their physical development. Building trust between practitioner and the parent is fundamental – every parent needs to know their child will be safe when they leave them in someone else's care. Responding sensitively to the needs of a very anxious parent can make a world of difference to the way that child (and their parent) will ultimately settle in.

For a child like Jake with Down's Syndrome, there is every reason to expect that he will benefit from mainstream education, not least because it allows him the opportunity to attend his local school and maintain local friendships. Australian studies have identified the important role of friendships in children's well-being and supporting transitions in particular (Margetts 1997). The first scenario builds on this while also ensuring that the boy's individuality is acknowledged. The second scenario denies Jake a level of implicit support that will be just as influential as any explicit support he gets for his 'special needs'.

The practitioner responses for Carl in the first scenario are a perfect example of the key person approach working well. Tuning into the child, getting to know his likes and dislikes and his strengths and motivations makes sure that his early experiences are tailored to suit him best and help the settling process. Carl is experiencing a degree of control over the activities in which he takes part, alongside the support of an adult gently encouraging and supporting him to engage in less familiar tasks. Information about the languages a child speaks at home together with his level of developing English is crucial to have at the outset (for a child of any age). Poor practice of the kind described in the second scenario is not good enough in any situation, but in this instance denies Carl the opportunity for important second language experiences as well as adding to his confusion and damaging his self-image.

For Kyle and his mother, his free place at a local nursery was a potential lifeline. Sensitive professional support for his mother, in the first instance, set out to encourage and ensure his attendance and in the long term would have provided her with much-needed support and guidance. Although Leanne's needs were extreme, the practitioners in the first scenario were able to bridge the divide between home and nursery by valuing mum and gently challenging her negative expectations, even before Kyle had been admitted. In the second scenario, the school failed Kyle (with devastating consequences) by being needlessly inflexible and, ultimately, professionally negligent.

All children benefit from consistency and predictability in early routines. They provide reassurance and also help the child build an image of the world around them and how it works. For a child like Jordie, those routines are an important part of his 'survival' – children on the autistic spectrum can find change particularly challenging. Sudden changes to routine, or haphazard timetables, are not helpful to young children in general, and in Jordie's case can be extremely threatening. The heightened stress for his mum impacts on their relationship as well as her ability to settle Jordie into school calmly. The fact that Jordie has been in school for some time does not mean that the impact of his transition has lessened in any way. The lack of predictability has just intensified and lengthened the settling process.

These are just a few examples of the kinds of children and their families who are 'extra vulnerable' at transition times. The specifics of the additional support any of them will need at varying times will be different depending on their individual circumstances. The point to stress here, however, is that good quality practice for *them* translates as good quality practice for *everyone*.

Horizontal transitions

The scenarios above mostly refer to vertical transitions – the kind that take place when there is a move from home to, or within, EYFS settings – but as already mentioned, our youngest children are also exposed to horizontal transitions throughout the day and these can have just as negative an impact on well-being. A child in full daycare may experience staff changes, shifts from room to room for

REFLECTION TASK

Have a think about ... feeling emotionally and physically dependent on others for your personal care.

Think about a time when you were ill either at home or in hospital. Did you experience any of these?

- Waiting for someone to come and provide you with food, or help you wash and dress?
- Being handled gently by some people, but more roughly and with less sensitivity by others?
- Dealing with different nurses, doctors or relatives and having to repeat your symptoms and explain your needs, over and over again?
- In hospital, feeling comfortable with a particular nurse or doctor who then changed their shift pattern or went on holiday?
- Being told you were making a fuss and making life difficult for people, or did you feel listened to and treated with empathy?
- Having procedures done that you didn't understand, by people who didn't interact with you and talked about you as if you weren't there?
- Watching people coming and going, getting on with their daily lives while you stayed in one place?

What emotions did the experience provoke, and how did it make you feel about yourself?

Unhappy?	Uncomfortable?	A nuisance?
Bemused?	Angry?	Helpless?
Frustrated?	Anxious?	Resigned?
Powerless?	Unsure of yourself?	Miserable?

Connect with those feelings for a minute or two. Now put yourself in the shoes of a small child in your setting who is effectively powerless to make decisions about their personal care.

Is it possible they will be handled with variable physical expertise and sensitivity and have little or no control over:

- how and when their nappy is changed/hands and face washed/ clothes changed etc., and by whom?
- the number of adults and children they have to interact with in a day?
- access to familiar places, people, toys and food?
- the quality of the interactions and relationships with the adults dealing with their physical care?

As adults, it is right that we hold the power in these situations, but we also have the responsibility of making sure we use this power with sensitivity and affectionate care.

This exercise adapted from Thorp and Manning Morton (2006).

different parts of the day as well as a variety of different people attending to their personal needs. Throughout that time, they are physically and emotionally dependent on the adults around them.

Parents and practitioners get stressed too

Now let's refer back to the scenarios one last time. Reread the negative list, but from the point of view of the parent and the practitioners involved.

■ What are the implications for the relationships being built with those parents?

■ How might their stress levels impact on their relationships with their children as well as with the practitioners?

■ What impact do these stressful situations have on the practitioners and their relationships with the children and families?

■ How might this impact on the practitioners' ability to get the best from these children in terms of early learning?

■ How does the stress of settling children affect the quality of the practitioner's working day?

And now read the positive scenarios with this same perspective.

Bearing in mind the negative and positive scenarios, I'll just ask two simple questions here.

■ Which would you rather your child experienced?

■ Which would you rather find yourself working in?

How much nicer is it to work in a genuinely caring environment that takes time, shows respect, offers a warm welcome and displays a flexible attitude?

As well as making the work situation better – let's face it, relaxed, happy children and parents are easier to work with – practitioners also benefit from the feel-good chemicals induced by positive interactions as well as a sense of job satisfaction and a pleasant working environment. The work we do is undeniably hard and complex, but an atmosphere of mutual respect and warmth, together with a shared sense of belonging, not only makes it feel easier – it should also reassure us that the same care and respect is likely to be given to our own needs and emotional well-being.

Empathy with parents

Bearing all of this in mind, let's look more closely at ways in which empathy with parents and families can improve the quality of experience for children. Sadly, many parents bringing their child to a setting for the first time may have uncomfortable memories of their own experiences of education or childcare. We need to be aware of this and think carefully about how we make our settings more welcoming – and less threatening – to new parents.

This means a lot more than a 'welcome' poster in the front entrance! Once again we need to use our powers of empathy to put ourselves in their shoes and look at our environment (and its policies and ethos) from the point of view of someone coming new to it. Encouraging a parent to be fully involved in settling their child can help to reduce their levels of anxiety while enabling them to get a good feel for the setting and how it works.

This isn't always possible, though, for working or time-limited parents, so we have to be creative and thoughtful in the way we do it. Perhaps a working parent might have more time at the end of the day when they come to pick up their child, rather than at the beginning. Home time might provide a much better opportunity for sitting and looking at books or playing in the home corner or sand tray. Factor in time for this if you can, and let parents know they don't always have to rush off.

Elfer, Goldschmied and Selleck (2012:90) refer to the 'triangle of trust and attachments' within the key person approach that includes the parents as well as the child. Creating that relationship by tuning into a parent's needs, recognising their unique enthusiasms and motivations, their skills and strengths as well as their anxieties and concerns is fundamental to the success of the approach.

An understanding of attachment theory helps us relate to the ways that individual parents might respond in their own ways to the stress of their child's transitions. It's fairly easy (though exhausting sometimes) to relate to an anxious parent's worries about their child, perhaps expressed in lots of questions, and the need for constant reassurance. Harder, perhaps, to appreciate that a parent who briskly waves their child goodbye, insisting they will be fine, has also found a way of handling their anxiety and might be just as much in need of sensitive support.

Hearing it from someone who has recently been in same situation

This is one of the most useful ways of showing empathy with someone who is experiencing transition, and perhaps we don't always give credit to how well children can provide this for each other. The work of the pre-schools in Reggio Emilia in Italy shows us how effective it can be to involve children in this process. They have produced a book, *Advisories* (Vecchi and Strozzi 2002), filled with the recollections and advice that five- and six-year-olds preparing to leave pre-school chose to provide for the incoming three-year-olds – how to find the toilets, which teacher wears make-up and which one is likely to pinch some of your dinner at lunchtime! They also talk openly about the things that concerned them.

■ 'Don't be afraid of school because there's nothing to be afraid of, because you get bigger and you like it.'

- 'When I came into this school I didn't know anybody, so I was scared and I thought "How can I get to know them?" First I made one friend and then together we got to know everybody.'

Who better to provide us with information about something new and potentially scary than someone who has just been through the same experience themselves? As the teachers comment at the beginning of the book, it is not a standard description of the pre-school: 'Rather it is an image that recreates the school by way of a strongly interpreted story of places and people. More than describing, it transforms the spaces, times, people and events of the school into small and big adventures of life' (Vecchi and Strozzi 2002:5).

In the Afterword, Sergio Spaggiari comments that the children's advice is neither 'consoling, nor alarming', and ensures that they neither 'frighten nor reassure them too much'. He notes that 'the extraordinary aspect of *Advisories* lies in the adults having credited five year old children not only with knowing how to reconstruct their own memory, but above all knowing how to re-propose it to an audience of younger children. The older children are implicitly asked to put themselves in the shoes of someone they do not know and contemplate their expectations and needs.' (Vecchi and Strozzi 2002:45).

A glossy book might be well outside our budget these days, but I think we should definitely take on board the idea and motivations behind *Advisories* and encourage our children leaving the Early Years Foundation Stage to tell it like it is – and we need to pay good attention to what they tell us.

Parents too can be the best people to inform new parents about what to expect and how best to handle situations new to them. Chapter 6 explores this aspect of supporting transitions in greater depth.

Summary

This chapter aimed to put the theoretical aspects of transition into real-life contexts as well as allowing adults the opportunity to put themselves in the shoes of the child and consider their own reactions to change and transition.

- Change and transition induce mixed emotions in all of us.

- What's important for us as adults during change is also important for children and their families.

- Ultimately a sense of belonging and feeling like a 'fish in water' is central to the idea of a good transition.

- All children and families are vulnerable during times of transition – although some are more vulnerable than most due to particular circumstances. Keeping the latter in mind when devising policies and practice is essential, as good practice for the most vulnerable amounts to good practice for all.

- Having enough of the 'positive stuff':

- builds a sense of familiarity and security (as the child repeats the regulation cycle)
- makes connections in the brain and builds neural pathways
- raises the level of 'feel-good chemicals' and keeps the stress chemicals low
- allows us to make the most of all parts of our brain and to move from 'reptilian' into 'thinking' brain more readily when we experience perceived threat during the transition process
- builds healthy resilience for future experiences of transition.

■ 'Settling' new children is a complex and challenging task that requires patience, insight and sensitivity.

■ Involving parents and children as much as possible builds reassurance and confidence in the transition process. They are also the best people to help inform and support other new parents and children.

■ Change and transition takes place on a daily basis for many children, and these horizontal transitions need just as much attention as the vertical transitions that take place when children move from stage to stage in early childhood.

Implications for practice

Supporting the secure primary attachments of all children, and particularly those in vulnerable families, has to be a main goal of our practice. Developing good secondary attachments is fundamental to this.

We need to:

■ recognise the child and family's entitlement to the same degree of care and attention that we would want for ourselves

■ reflect critically on the lack of choice and control we allow children in the changes they experience and the ways in which they would choose to deal with change (this is true of horizontal as well as vertical transition)

■ find ways to ensure that our settling and transition procedures are flexible, empathic and respectful of the individual needs of children and families

■ act professionally to challenge routines and procedures that don't support continuity of attachments

■ pay attention to our own stress at 'settling' times, building mutual support into the admission and transition process.

CHAPTER

5

Strategies for reducing transitions in the early years

This chapter takes account of the fact that though many babies and young children continue to be cared for outside of the home, it is still possible to reduce the number of transitions, both horizontal and vertical, that children experience. Starting with a consideration of Richard Bowlby's model of 'attachment-based daycare', it is easy to see the value of childminding as perhaps the optimum outcome for babies and young children needing daycare. It makes sense then, to explore how elements of the childminding model can be used to inform practice in settings.

By looking at the steps taken by some local authorities and individual settings, this chapter provides both examples of good practice and points to consider when exploring possible solutions. It also examines the key person approach, highlighting its importance in supporting attachment and the crucial role it can play (if practised well) in reducing the impact of transitions, both horizontal and vertical, within settings.

Essential features of 'attachment-based daycare'

Richard Bowlby has outlined what he believes to be the only desirable form of childcare outside the home. He describes it as 'attachment-based daycare' and emphasises that it is only suitable for babies of nine months or older, making the point that this allows time for the child to have formed an attachment bond with their primary carer. Care for babies should be part-time until they are at least 18 months old, and carers should have no more than three babies or toddlers, well spaced in age:

- one child 9–18 months
- one child 18–36 months
- one child over 36 months.

The initial separation must be gradual and the duration of the care session must be kept short during the early stages to ensure, as much as possible, that cortisol levels are not raised. The child's parent (primary attachment figure) stays with the child for the first stage while the baby 'makes friends' with the new carer.

Other essential features of the model include:

■ continuity of personalised care for several years

■ the carer makes an emotional commitment to the child

■ family-type grouping allows age-appropriate care for each child

■ carers actively encourage children to form secondary attachments to them

■ parents are supported to understand and sanction this secondary attachment bond

■ carers are well trained and supported to meet the physical, intellectual and emotional challenges of caring for babies and young children, and their emotional attachment to the children they care for is sensitively supported and monitored.

This all helps to ensure that:

■ Babies' and toddlers' secondary attachment needs are always met, maintained and monitored.

■ Parents are supported in maintaining their child's primary attachment to them (R. Bowlby 2007).

The value of childminders

Childminders are able to provide a level of personalised and sustained care for children in a way that is difficult to replicate in group daycare provision. They have fewer children and the span of ages better reflects the natural grouping of a family. Children will often receive daycare from the same childminder from the date when the parent returns to work right through until the child starts school, often continuing to receive before- and after-school and holiday care for several years more.

Policy and legislation for childminding provide a framework for this optimum type of care that attempts to regulate and maintain standards and quality. However, elements of the EYFS (and registration and inspection procedures) have 'bureaucratised' the role of the childminder and added layers of paperwork to an already demanding job. There is no denying that increased legislation and registration requirements have provided essential safeguards and have raised the status of childminding to that of a profession – albeit one that charges an average of only £3.90 per hour per child (Evans 2011). But it can also inhibit people from registering and benefiting from much-needed support. As self-employed

individuals, childminders can feel isolated and struggle to replicate some of the extensive learning opportunities that settings can provide.

Children's Centres can provide a base for a range of services for registered childminders (as Service Level Agreements with the National Childminding Association, for example), offering facilities for meeting, training, vacancy matching, etc., but it remains a fact that there are many carers who choose not to seek registration.

Co-ordinated childminding

Richard Bowlby wrote in 2007 about a model for co-ordinated childminding that addressed this situation and also brought together the best of both worlds of childminding and group care. It involved:

- seven or eight self-employed individuals each caring for three children under five (only one under 18 months) and paid directly by the parents
- working collectively under the supervision of a co-ordinator
- in a designated space within a local Family or Children's Centre.

This allowed carers that might otherwise have found it challenging to register as childminders to provide personalised care over a period of years in a mutually supportive and guided environment. The benefits to the children (and families) lay in the quality and intimacy of the personalised care that could be sustained without interruption until the child transferred to school, as well as the opportunity for socialising and playing in a well-equipped environment. The guidance of the co-ordinator ensured the quality of care and provision and empowered the carers to develop their skills and experience.

Ofsted's annual report of 2009/10, commenting on the difference between the proportion of childcare providers on non-domestic premises rated as good or outstanding (nearly three quarters) and that of childminders (two thirds) noted that:

> It may be the case that childcare providers on non-domestic premises benefit from working routinely with other practitioners and are therefore able to exchange ideas, share their practice and identify common areas for improvement, whereas the childminders, who often work alone, may not have such opportunities.
>
> (Ofsted, cited in Evans 2011)

It would seem that the model above would do much to address this situation. Sadly, it is not the cheapest way of providing childcare and would probably now be impossible given current legal requirements. And yet from the point of view of secure secondary attachments for children and sustained support for carers, it would be hard to beat it.

Shared care in childminding

Some registered childminders are able to choose not to work in isolation, however, and there is increasing evidence of two or more childminders working together (often within families) to create childminding partnerships. Writing in response to an article about paired and shared key caring in the *Journal of Early Education* (Spring 2008), Ruth and Leslie Miller describe their way of working together as a 'unit'. They keep the number of children below that allowed by their individual registrations in order to ensure flexibility and 'back-up'. They are able jointly to meet the needs of the children by sharing the care between them and eating and playing together, but they are also able to accommodate individual needs by doing separate things in response to the children's requirements, e.g. one takes the older children to the park while the other stays at home with the youngest who are sleeping.

They comment on the advantages of this way of working for them as well as the children:

> Working together certainly eases the stress of the constant demands of working with young children. We are both equally involved in the care of our children but we do also play to each other's strengths. I am a retired teacher with many years' experience in early years. Leslie is a retired television engineer, and his engineering mind brings an unprecedented quality to children's play. The children move between us, and with us, in an easy and natural manner as the routine of each day proceeds.
>
> (Miller and Miller 2008)

REFLECTION TASK

If you are a childminder, have a think about . . .

- What do you think you need to know about attachment theory and the development of the brain?
- How do you make sure that you get enough support for your role as an important secondary attachment figure for the children in your care?
- How do you support children's primary attachment? How do you support parents' attachment to their children?
- Can you access services and resources at your local Children's Centre?
- Are you able to work collectively with other carers to benefit the children?

REFLECTION TASK

If you are a practitioner or manager, have a think about . . .

- What can you learn from the childminder's way of working?
- What other ways of grouping children are you aware of that are different to the way your current setting is organised?
- Are there places you can visit?

There are always pros and cons with every system of organisation. Critically reflect on how the organisation of your setting:

- *supports* primary and secondary attachments
- *creates* transitions for children
- *reduces* transitions or keeps them manageable.

Removing transitions by age or stage

The childminder model promotes sustained, personalised care over an extended period of time, ideally several years. Steiner's focus on relationships led him to suggest too that children should stay with the same teacher for a number of years. This is an element that has been explored outside of the Steiner system, both in the 'vertical grouping' approach used in some primary schools and in some nurseries where 'family' or 'open-age' grouping is used to good effect. This allows children of different ages to be grouped together and remain as a core group with the same practitioners for two to three years. It is also a regular occurrence in small rural schools where there is no option other than to group children across the age bands.

Other schools may not have a policy as such for this to happen, but are open to classes remaining with the same teacher over a two year period when particular circumstances arise. The general consensus of opinion among practitioners who have experienced this is that the strengthened relationships that develop have a profound impact on the emotional well-being and academic progress of the children, and that classes that have previously experienced disruption and lots of change (e.g. through teacher absence) often benefit from a prolonged period of stability over and above the usual yearly transition.

Family grouping and open or multi-age nursery settings

While they are not common, there are increasing numbers of settings exploring the potential of grouping across age ranges. Although grouping children by age was originally seen as providing a better way of meeting developmental needs, many practitioners and early years specialists find that the opposite is true. A balance of ages makes it easier to meet individual needs and the breadth of expectation means that there are no narrow perceptions of what children should – or shouldn't – be doing at any given age. Lilian Katz, writing in 1995 about the benefits of mixed-age groups, commented that 'Although humans are not usually born in litters, we seem to insist that they be educated in them'.

In any typical family grouping (which is, after all, the original and most natural way of raising and caring for children), it would be rare to have more than two children of the same age at any one time, and they generally arrive as singles at least nine months apart. And yet even in childcare, we see the 'school' model holding sway, of grouping children by chronological year group.

In the mixed-age model, the children don't move 'up' from one room (or part of the setting) to the next because of a birthday, or a gap in numbers. They interact on a regular basis with babies and children of all ages, often with greater access to all the space available. There are some clear benefits to this. As well as removing the stress and upheaval of transition, it reinforces relationships and allows children the opportunity not just to learn from older peers but also to have the chance to nurture and care for those younger than them. This is exactly the kind of experience believed to be absent for many children in today's smaller and generally more isolated nuclear families, and is directly linked to their eventual understanding of nurture and child rearing.

Working with mixed ages isn't without its challenges, and there is still a need for vigilance to make sure that younger children aren't overwhelmed or their needs overlooked. There has to be a degree of flexibility in making it work for everyone, by allowing some separation when needed. But this is about attunement and knowing what is right for individual children at different times – and a good setting will always build in flexibility to its policies to ensure this. There are a range of ways to adapt and organise for flexibility, depending on the limitations of environment and staffing etc. Some settings will provide a separate but linked space for babies to rest or have a quiet time. Others will have mixed-age groups but in clearly defined spaces for 'under threes' and 'over threes', with just one transition between the two.

Vertical grouping in nurseries: a proprietor's perspective

Bents Farm Nursery, Halifax, is an example of an 'open-age' private nursery that does not organise children by age groups. The children have access to all rooms, including the base room for the babies. However, the babies also have a room in which they can sleep undisturbed and the environment (both inside and out) can be organised so that a group of children can work on a project undisturbed when necessary. This flexibility ensures that the needs of one group of children don't override or compete with the needs of another.

The children's developmental stage and experience are considered when organising any group activities, rather than their age. The setting uses a key person approach and the proprietor is active in the setting on a daily basis to support this. It has been running this way since 2008 and is staffed above the minimum requirements, to ensure it works well. Although some new parents of babies have initial anxieties about safety, they are reassured by the quality of the practice and come to realise that the approach has many benefits, particularly for first or only children who don't have opportunities to be around children of different ages.

The proprietor, Julie White, comments on the increase in empathy shown by children towards each other and the high levels of confidence and independence in children making the transition to school. With regard to the 'under threes' she observes, 'I can see them venturing off and making their own little transitions – of what they play with and where they play – but this is all done naturally as their need arises. It's a natural progression for them, without adult intervention. They all get to the same place, but mine get there without the stress' (Julie White 2011).

Vertical grouping in schools: a practitioner's perspective

Tricia Carroll, Senior Lecturer in Early Years and English at the University of Cumbria, reflects on her experience as an infant teacher working with a vertically grouped class of five- to seven-year-olds in the early 1980s.

I'm not sure I knew the motivation behind the decision for this school to group the children vertically – it may have been done because of falling rolls. But for the children, it was a happy accident of history. It meant I worked with them (and their families) for three whole years. I knew them so well.

It worked like an apprenticeship model whereby my top infants (Y2) supported and modelled for my younger ones. As I remember it, new reception children settled quickly. They would be a relatively small group, making it easier for me to give them my attention (unlike a class full of new reception children all settling at the same time) and with so many 'siblings' to watch out for them and show them the ropes, it made for a very calm and unpressured environment. I don't remember ever thinking that meeting the needs of different ages within the same class was a problem. Indeed, I felt that I was really able to respond to individual needs. Having each little age group stay with me for three years meant that there was no interruption to their flow at the beginning of each school year – we just picked up where we left off. I knew the children and their families well and there were no transitions for them to deal with until they transferred to the junior school at age seven.

(Tricia Carroll 2012)

Vertical grouping in schools: a parent's perspective

Della Clark's children attended a very small rural school with one infant and one junior class. They both started school in the September a few months after their fourth birthdays.

It worked well for the girls, they benefited from having older children around who were quite mature and helpful and they settled quickly. They got to know their teacher really well and they didn't have to cope with getting to know a new one every year or moving to a new classroom. Everything was familiar to them so there was no disruption when they went back to school after the long summer holidays.

(Della Clark 2012)

Vertical grouping in schools: a child's perspective

I enjoyed being in the company of a mixed-age group, especially my older peers, who I looked up to. I also enjoyed helping out with the little ones, I was able to relate to them, they looked up to me just as I had looked up to someone like me. The teachers had become friends by the time I left, just with more authority. This helped me in the learning process as my teachers knew me well and could relate topics to things I was interested in. However, because there was such a small number of us, we all had to get on well. Also having to leave a school of 30 pupils and start another school of 1300 pupils was very daunting.

(Mia Clark 2012)

Challenges of vertical grouping

Practitioners working with a mixed age range in this way have to be particularly skilful in meeting the needs of all the children and their many stages of development. They need to be confident in their understanding of the full breadth of the curriculum and see themselves as specialists in not just one age group but two or three! Transitions do occur, however, as whenever a member of staff leaves, they will be midway through the process for at least one group of children.

Despite the practice of vertical grouping being commonplace in small rural schools, it seems to have very much fallen out of favour everywhere else. Perhaps an increased understanding and appreciation of the importance of attachment and relationships in children's well-being and brain development might trigger a new perspective on this approach?

Foundation Stage Units

One way of addressing the significant transition from nursery to reception is to remove it altogether! If the Early Years Foundation Stage includes the reception year, why do we still consider it appropriate to create a break within the age group? The development of Foundation Stage or EYFS Units (or Early Years Units as they were known before the existence of the EYFS) was a move to challenge this notion. An increasing number of local authorities and individual schools are developing provision in this way, although the title FSU may in fact be used to describe a range of different organisational structures.

Depending on the degree of integration, nursery and reception provision in an FSU might be:

- closely linked
- combined for parts of the day
- completely integrated throughout the day.

In some cases the nursery provision will be maintained, but increasingly the nursery element is likely to be private or voluntary provision.

In these settings, children and their families naturally increase their familiarity with staff and the environment. In units where the children are completely integrated from the ages of three to five plus, there is no transition to be negotiated. Children will spend a minimum of two years with the same staff, in the same environment, and there is no break to their progress through the EYFS curriculum. Practitioners are able to build strong relationships with children and their families over the two years, helping to build greater attunement to children's needs and stronger partnerships with families (O'Connor 2006).

Local authority support for Foundation Stage Units

Devon County Council encourages the development of FSUs with a recognised badging scheme. As well as offering support with curriculum and operational issues, the optional badging process provides a four-phase process that has the monitoring of quality at its core.

FSUs operate in a range of ways:

- *fully integrated* – both providers share the same internal and external physical space
- *semi-integrated* – the physical space has the potential to accommodate fully integrated practice but providers choose to work independently for all or part of the day
- *parallel* – the physical restriction of two separate buildings or rooms prevents full integration
- *mixed phase* – the Foundation Stage Unit includes children under three and in Key Stage 1 or both, and may operate as A, B or C, so is particularly suitable for smaller schools (www.devon.gov.uk/eycs-schools-fsu?nocache=8118, accessed 6 February 2012).

Where the nursery/pre-school provision element is private or voluntary then the unit is designated as a Partnership Foundation Stage Unit (PFSU). There are greater challenges in this process as there are different Ofsted requirements and working practices to be managed cohesively, but the benefits are the same. As well as the reduction of stress around transitions, PFSU and FSU practitioners report increased opportunities for shared expertise, better access to resources and the positive aspect of feeling less isolated from other age groups.

(Fran Butler, Early Years Development Manager and Sheena Wright, Lead Early Years Quality and Inclusion Adviser, Devon County Council 2011)

The benefits of a fully integrated Foundation Stage Unit

My own experience of setting up and developing an early years unit (EYU) in the early 1990s confirmed for me the importance of 'protecting' reception age children from formal schooling and of removing the artificial boundary between three- to four-year-old children and those who were four to five years of age. The move grew from a clear conviction on the part of the local authority early years advisers of the value of extending the pedagogy and quality of the 'nursery' experience into the reception class.

Children in a fully integrated FSU really do have a seamless transition from nursery into reception. There is no change to their environment, the structure of their day or the adults who work with them. They return in the September for their second year as 'old hands' ready to welcome and support the new children. They are relaxed and enthusiastic about revisiting familiar experiences. They are confident in this secure and familiar place yet eager to extend and develop their skills as they stretch and challenge themselves further with no uncertainty to hold them back.

Along with that security goes a sense of themselves as 'older' – of being the 'big ones' – with a level of responsibility and capability that is a far cry from the experience of being 'brand new' in the reception class. At the same time, those older children who need longer to explore experiences and assimilate early concepts can do so in an environment that continues to meet them 'where they're at', because the practitioners working with them are already well attuned to their individual stage of development and the environment is broad enough to accommodate their needs. Differentiation by outcome enables children of different ages and experience levels to participate in shared activities, using the same resources but arriving at different outcomes, supported by practitioners who know them well enough to provide challenge as well as reassurance and support.

Younger children benefit from the support of older ones, and less experienced children (of any age) benefit from the opportunity to work at their own pace alongside more experienced role models. Older children benefit from being able to help and care for younger children. Siblings can support each other, and spend time playing together as well as time apart following their own interests. Attachments and relationships with children and their parents are stronger over the two year period and families are more confident about their own role in the school community. And when the time comes to make the transition into Y1, the children are more resilient and 'ready' for what comes next. They are ready to move on – and as practitioners we feel more confident about letting them go, knowing that they have had the time to consolidate as well as develop their new skills and learning.

Creating a 'transition space'

Some settings allow pre-school children timetabled access to a space also used by children already in the reception class. The room provides a 'transition space' that builds familiarity among the younger children and allows the older children to revisit an environment with which they were previously familiar. It also allows the children the opportunity to mix with children of a similar age, but who would otherwise be chronologically separated. Some settings have found that providing a flexible 'halfway house' in this way can be very helpful to children. It is particularly useful in providing the reception children with the opportunity to revisit and return to a familiar space and keep their links with children and staff from the nursery while they adjust to life in their new environment.

Here are two examples of transition spaces in Children's Centres:

The Rainbow Room at Westgate Primary School and Children's Centre

This connects the three reception classes to the private daycare nursery. A self-registration, free-flow system is used with all pre-school and reception children within certain periods of the morning and afternoon. The room provides age-appropriate continuous provision. Reception teachers, classroom assistants (experienced nursery nurses) and preschool key people all work within this room. This provides the reception children with opportunities to see their old key person regularly and the pre-school children who will attend the primary school also have the opportunity to meet their future class teacher and classroom assistants.

This response to children's need to revisit familiar spaces is just as important for younger children.

West View Garden space at Rising Stars Nursery, Firbank Children's Centre

The 'under threes' area in this nursery is separate from the 'over threes' space, but the garden for the children in Plum Tree room (two to threes) has a door that links it to the Apple Tree (three to fours) room. When numbers and staffing allow, the children who have moved on are some-times able to return to this space, revisiting people and activities they are familiar with. This smaller, contained space can also provide a retreat from the much larger outdoor environment designed for the older children, which will benefit some children during the transition process, who are still getting used to the challenge and stimulation of their new outdoor area.

These are just a few examples of strategies that help to reduce the impact of vertical transitions within the early years foundation stage. They are not without their challenges, but the settings themselves are clear about the benefits. In the case of some, they have had to go against the tide of customary practice in order to develop provision that challenges the usual way of doing things. Where the practice is widespread across a local authority, with advisory support, training and clear guidance, it is ultimately easier – and less risky – to change current practice and develop new and better ways of organisation. In time, it becomes the norm – and staff and families wonder why they ever thought it was acceptable to function in any other way.

Unfortunately, where the support is not available, it can be difficult to maintain a new conceptual way of working in the face of opposition from policy-makers (locally and at government level) who do not fully understand the issues involved.

REFLECTION TASK

Have another think about . . .

What changes are possible within your current setting?

- It may be that major changes are just not possible – although it is still worth holding onto a vision of how you would like things to be.
- Are there small changes that would make a difference to the quality of a child's transition into, within, or moving on from your setting?
- What support will you need to carry through any changes?

This is particularly so when a drive towards 'school readiness' is at the heart of government plans for the early years, ignoring all evidence and inevitably pushing for an earlier start to formal education. Happily there are local authorities that appreciate the value of pedagogical initiatives that reduce the stress of transition and safeguard the special nature of the early years foundation stage.

Key people

One of the most fundamental ways of addressing both horizontal and vertical transitions is through the key person approach.

> Since the 1990s, the key worker or person approach has steadily become established across the UK as a strong recommendation for group provision. Descriptions of this approach were part of national and local early years guidance. In England, the birth to five framework of the Early Years Foundation Stage (EYFS) moved from the level of recommendation of the key person system into a non-negotiable requirement.
>
> (Lindon 2010:5)

Sadly this hasn't always meant that the approach has been understood or managed effectively. There are many reasons for this and Elfer et al. explore these in depth, together with the issues raised against the use of the approach, in the 2012 revised edition of *Key Persons in the Early Years: Building relationships for quality provision in early years settings and primary schools*. They summarise the arguments against the key person approach as follows.

1. It brings staff too close to a parental role and they risk becoming over-involved.
2. If children get too close to any one member of staff, it is painful for them if that member of staff is not available.
3. It can be threatening for parents who may be jealous of a special relationship between their child and another adult.

4. The key person approach is complex to organise and staff need to work as a team, not as individuals.

5. It undermines the opportunities for children to participate in all the relationships of the early years setting community (Elfer et al. 2012:10–11).

An understanding of attachment theory, early brain structure and child develop-ment, however, suggests that though these arguments reflect real issues and genuine feelings and emotions likely to be triggered by the approach, they do not justify the consequences for babies and young children left to cope with serial, impersonalised care. Elfer et al. are very clear about this: 'Overall, we think the evidence about the nature of human relationships and the longing to form individual attachments, particularly for very young children, is so overwhelming that the arguments to do with feelings and organisation given above become challenges to be overcome rather than reasons *not* to develop the Key Persons approach' (2012:11; emphasis in original).

They are also clear about the difference between a 'key worker', who has an organisational or co-ordination responsibility liaising between various professionals and disciplines, and a 'key person', who is much, much more. 'The essence of the key person role is to be someone who is "key" to the child . . . [and] has real daily meaning and emotional significance to the child and his family' (Elfer et al. 2012:24). This is why they refer to it as an 'approach' rather than a 'system'.

The key person approach and secondary attachments

Veronica Read comments on the central role of the key person in promoting attachment in early years settings.

> When the key person approach is truly valued for what it can become for both children, practitioners and parents, then we see attachment theory in practice. For it is through this thoughtful way of working with a small group of children, that staff have their best opportunity of conveying to a child that their inner emotional states are known and shared – *affect attunement*. Staff who are available, attentive and attuned to infants and young children help them at times of separation and loss.
>
> (Read 2010:62–63; emphasis in original)

John Bowlby described four distinguishing characteristics of attachment:

■ **proximity maintenance** – the desire to be near the people we are attached to

■ **safe haven** – returning to the attachment figure for comfort and safety in the face of a fear or threat

■ **secure base** – the attachment figure acts as a base of security from which the child can explore the surrounding environment

■ **separation distress** – anxiety that occurs in the absence of the attachment figure (J. Bowlby 1969, 1973, 1980).

Looking at an effective key person approach in the context of these four characteristics reinforces the way that practitioners in this role function as important
secondary attachment figures:

■ **proximity maintenance** – children seek out their key people, like to know
where they are and often stay close by them on arrival

■ **safe haven** – children look to their key people for comfort and reassurance
when sad, unhappy, ill or anxious

■ **secure base** – children branch out from their key people as they grow in
confidence and feel safe enough to explore

■ **separation distress** – children distressed by the separation from a parent will
allow themselves to be comforted by their key people. They will also
experience distress when separated from a key person, which is why it is
important to have pairs of key people or a 'back-up' person who knows the
child well.

Key person approach and transition

Let's look at the ways in which the key person approach helps reduce the impact
of transition in theory – and what must be in place to ensure that it works well
in practice.

Supported settling

One of the main expectations of the approach (even when used minimally) is that
the key person(s) will support the child (and parents) with the settling process. A
key person will have made a home visit and be there to greet the child on their
first and subsequent days. Through the information shared on the home visit they
will be familiar with the child's likes and dislikes, their interests and motivations
and the best ways to soothe them when they become distressed. They will be the
familiar face in the lively buzz of an early years setting first thing in the morning,
when there is lots going on and plenty of to-ing and fro-ing. They will be the
hand to hold, the lap to sit on and the arms to be cuddled in, when the time comes
to separate from mum or dad and when it all gets a bit too much to handle. They
will be there for the parents too – to soothe and reassure them and to fill them in
on everything they need to know about their child's day when they are away from
them.

Ongoing support

A key person isn't just there for the settling period, however – they are in it for
the long haul! Familiarity and consistency are important in reducing anxiety and
stress levels and the child is reassured by the continued presence of their key person.

This is just as important for the little changes that take place during the day, e.g. moving to a different room for lunch, coming to the carpet for a group time, getting ready to go home, as well as unscheduled changes such as fire alarms, photographer visits, assemblies, parties and performances. They are also responsible for the personal care routines of their key children, making the most of intimate moments for building relationship and connection.

Back up

Key people aren't superhuman, so they sometimes get sick or have holidays, and some children spend a longer day in the setting than the length of any practitioner's shift. Because of this, there needs to be a 'back-up' key person. This is a crucial part of the approach, and there are a few different ways of organising for it. Sally Thomas (2008) particularly advocates 'paired and shared key caring' where pairs of key people work together with shared key groups. Matching young practitioners with older, possibly more experienced practitioners not only supports professional development but also provides parents with the option, if they need it, of confiding in a key person that more closely matches their age (whichever it may be).

Other settings have a 'buddy' for each key group, or position the team leader or class teacher as co-key person for all the groups, getting to know all the children well, supporting and mentoring the key people and stepping in when one of them is unavailable. The important aspect is that the key person approach recognises the impact that missing someone can have on a child. The often unexplained absence of a practitioner, replaced with a supply teacher or agency staff, can have a huge impact on a child, unsettling them and damaging their confidence, leading to a range of behaviours as they try to communicate their distress. An effective key person approach minimises any potential damage by focusing on the quality of relationship, ensuring that practitioners do not work in isolation, and by providing that all-important 'back-up' when needed.

Building strong attachments and secure relationships

A true key person approach provides time and opportunity for relationship building, often in designated key group times as well as spontaneously throughout the day and during personal care routines. This is what makes it different to standard interactions with staff who may be familiar, but are not 'special', to the child and their family. These relationships are not just warm and affectionate, they are personalised and individual, signified by the particular levels of attunement that the adult gains with the child. These relationships are all-important when it comes to transitions – they build resilience and enable children to feel 'held in mind' when the time comes to move on.

Secure base

When these secure relationships are in place, the child will be able to branch out and take what John Bowlby referred to as a 'series of excursions' (Bowlby 1988) away from the key person. The secure base means there is someone to come running to when help is required or when things don't quite go according to plan. A practitioner who knows their key children well will recognise when they are ready to branch out into new relationships and challenges, but still be there for reassurance.

The key person approach doesn't restrict a child's ability to widen their social circle – it supports and sustains it.

> There is a subtle skilful balance to be made between helping a child have the confidence to be adventurous and stretch their capacities (whether taking on the challenge of an activity alone or tentatively forging new relationships with other children) from a secure base with their key person, and trying to force the child to do these things by not allowing him to have a secure base with his key person in the first place.
>
> (Elfer et al. 2012)

The secure base provided by their key people supports the child through the various daily transitions with which they have to deal when they are away from home.

Relationships with parents

Just as important in the key person approach is the bond with the child's parent(s). Partnership with parents has long been advocated but it doesn't always translate into meaningful practice. However, remembering that support for *primary* as well as *secondary* attachments lies at the heart of the key person approach can help to throw light on this tricky subject and reinforce the importance of the relationship between key people and the family.

At times of transitions and separation in particular, parents will need reassurance and sensitivity to their individual ways of handling change and separation. Share with parents the ways that you help the child to 'hold them in mind' as well as to feel 'held in mind' by the people most important to them. Think carefully too about the comments you make to reassure parents. What is more comforting to hear – 'she was fine the minute you left' or 'she missed you but settled well after a few minutes'? (O'Connor 2008).

Key people moving with their key group

This is an approach that carefully addresses transition by enabling the key person to make the internal move (from one stage to another) with their key group of children. Jennie Lindon (2010) refers to this as a 'travelling key group' and describes the advantages as well as the challenges this approach can bring. She notes that 'it offers continuity to children and families. Neither the child, nor the parent(s) have to develop a relationship with the new key person, probably at least twice in a birth to five years range nursery or centre' (Lindon 2010:28). However, such groups 'can raise difficulties for balancing the staff team and the point at which a practitioner returns to the beginning of the age range' (Lindon 2010:29). It also means that staff have to become skilled across the entire age range, which although useful, doesn't allow for particular specialism.

Key people in reception classes

As the requirement for a key person is an obligation throughout the EYFS, they need to be in place in reception classes too. Regardless of whether primary school managers and staff understand and value the approach, there is an obvious difficulty, in that adult–child ratios in reception classes are less than favourable. It is rare these days (thankfully) that a teacher finds themselves working alone with 30 four- to five-year-olds, but even one extra adult (usually a teaching assistant, less often an NNEB or other qualified early years practitioner) entails the child moving from a relatively small key group relationship in nursery to sharing their key person with at least 14 others. Where there are two assistants in the class, there is the option to have key groups of 10, or alternatively to give each assistant a key group and for the class teacher to provide the 'safety net' of a second person for each group. A good class teacher would always make strong relationships with all their children, but the special relationship the children make with their key people provides the class teacher with a level of insight and support for each child that they could not possibly achieve on their own.

As Dorothy Y. Selleck (2009) pointed out in her article outlining the then new EYFS requirements, primary school head teachers and early years staff needed to ensure that the main focus for key group times in reception classes was about

---

REFLECTION TASK

Have a think about . . . the key person approach in your setting

- Do all staff understand the principles behind the approach?
- Is there an effective back-up system to ensure that children always have a key person available to them?
- Do your transition policies reflect and support the significant nature of the key person approach?
- Do all staff working as key people receive mentoring and supervision? Do they have regular opportunities to reflect on their work and the children in their key group, to discuss concerns and to 'offload' to an experienced colleague so that the intense responsibilities of their role do not become too overwhelming?

building close relationships through 'real reciprocal conversations' and the need to 'counter any pressures for key times to be eclipsed by adult-led teaching targets, standards or assessments' (Selleck 2009:4).

Challenges to improve adult–child ratios in reception classes in response to consultations on the EYFS seem, so far, to have gone unheeded. This may be outside of our control currently, but it is an important issue and one we must continue to highlight.

Summary

There are a variety of organisational ways to reduce or manage the number of transitions experienced by young children. They all come with practical considerations but are worth bearing in mind because of their potential for reducing the impact of stress and interruption to learning and development caused by too many transitions at a young age. They include:

- promoting the value of childminders and models for their support and development
- removing transitions by age or stage and creating vertical or family groupings
- combining or integrating provision for nursery and reception
- providing 'transition spaces' for children to become familiar with new staff and to revisit staff and activities they knew previously
- the key person approach and the role it plays in supporting attachment, building resilience, providing continuity and the potential for reducing transition through 'travelling key groups' etc.

Implications for practice

- Despite the organisational challenges to be met when reducing transitions, there is a lot to be gained in the emotional health and well-being of children and the impact this ultimately has on their progress and development.
- Management and senior leadership need to be clear on the value and purposes of the key person approach and ensure that sufficient time, effort and resources are made available to assist key carers in their work and to ensure the effectiveness of the approach.
- Systems and organisation of key people and age groups etc. need regular review and adaptation to meet changing needs.
- Relationships with parents are critical, and organisational practices that support sustained reciprocal relationships over time between parents and practitioners have a positive impact on children's well-being and achievement.

6

Strategies to support children's well-being during transition

This chapter will draw together all the elements of the previous chapters and look at how we put theory into practice to support children's well-being during the transition process. We want to strike that balance between recognising the potential stress and difficulties that children might face during transition while also maximising the benefits and development potential that supported and appropriate transition to new environments can bring.

REFLECTION TASK

Have a think about . . . the best possible transition experience for a child in your setting.

What does it look like . . .

- for the child?
- for the child's family?
- for the practitioners working with that child?

Although there are specific aspects relating to particular ages and settings, it is worth being clear about the principles that should guide our approach to transition *of any kind and at any age*.

The goals of a good transition process

An ideal transition experience will enable every child

- to feel held in mind
- to feel like a fish in water
- to feel a sense of belonging.

All of which contribute to feelings of safety and unconditional acceptance, which will enable them

■ to feel ready, willing and able to make the most of the new situation.

These aims then need to be translated into policies and practice that are flexible enough to respond to the individual needs and circumstances of children and their families. It is rarely a case of 'one size fits all', but there are some working generalisations that can be helpful.

The settling process

In technical terms this is often described as the 'adaptation period'. As practitioners and parents we are much more likely to use the term 'settling'. *It is also the crucial time for the secondary attachment bond to begin developing.* Our understanding of the theories of attachment and transition, together with what we know about how young brains develop, would suggest that children who are settling (at any age and into any setting) do best when the following conditions are met.

Transition is made a priority

Managers, head teachers, proprietors and governing bodies need to show that they are aware of the importance of transition by making it a priority. There are time and cost implications in this, as there are in anything that improves the quality of experience for the child, although these are outweighed by the longer term benefits of happy, well-settled children, who are able to grow and achieve. It is up to us to be creative about how we achieve the best we can within the financial and organisational constraints that our current systems place upon us. It is also up to us not to use those constraints as excuses for not providing the best for our children.

Practitioners need time to be allowed to focus on the settling process as well as the initial stages of meeting children and their families, making home visits, gathering and transferring information, etc. We also need time to focus on how we build a curriculum and ethos that allow the gradual and supported integration of new children. All too often, it is the 'top-down' expectations, routines and organisational procedures that get in the way of practitioners really being able to respond to the individual needs of children who are coping with transition both into and out of the setting. Ideally, the settling process needs to be tuned to the needs of the child, with the parents and practitioners working together to share their understanding of how well the process fits what the child needs.

They are familiar with the people, places and routines

If familiarity is one of the most important factors supporting a smooth transition, then a one-off visit or introductory session is definitely not going to meet that

need. We need to look creatively at finding ways for children to become as familiar as possible with a new setting and its staff. Photo books and DVD films of the setting (see 'Prepare a welcome pack', p. 110) that can be borrowed and watched at home help consolidate the visits and give parents the chance to respond spontaneously to children's interest and their sometimes urgent desire for information!

They can make frequent visits to the setting

This is clearly useful in helping a child and their family become familiar with a new setting, but these visits need to be more than just the formal 'new admissions' visit or 'open day'. If we believe that uncertainty can heighten stress in some children and adults, then we need to find ways of reducing that uncertainty and increasing familiarity. Children benefit from frequent, informal drop-in opportunities with a parent, carer or familiar adult supporting them. These allow them to gain first-hand experience of the new setting at different times of the day and build familiarity with the environment as well as the people. The parent (or familiar adult who comes with them) provides the 'secure base' that allows them to take the risk of exploring and finding out about this new place and the people in it. The repetition of positive experiences not only helps reduce uncertainty but also builds positive associations with the new environment and the people and experiences they will meet there.

They receive a home visit

Home visiting needs to be approached with sensitivity and planned carefully to make sure it is beneficial. But the rewards will definitely make it worth the effort as it is a powerful opportunity to allow children (and families) to get to know practitioners on their own home ground. (See 'The importance of home visiting', p. 108.)

They are supported by key people

Children (and their parents or carers) arriving into the buzz and confusion of a new setting need to know they are not on their own. They need a guide and interpreter to help them make sense of this strange new world that they've found themselves in. A key person approach will ideally provide each child and their family with at least one key person together with an all-important 'back-up' person. This means that there will always be at least one very familiar person available to each child and family, even though they will also be interacting with other members of staff throughout their day.

They can build strong attachments and feel held in mind

Building warm, affectionate and secure relationships with significant people in one setting is the best protective factor for transition to another setting. Contrary to what was often believed in the past, becoming too attached to someone they have to leave is not the issue. Our increased understanding of attachment and its impact on the brain helps us to appreciate this. The solid foundation of a secure base provides a child with everything they need in order to be able to make the move to something less familiar. During the process of transition, they know they are held in mind by people who care about them – and can hold them in mind too – until they make strong attachments to the next important people in the next phase of their lives.

Their parents are involved, consulted and supported

It is important to recognise the potential stress and uncertainty experienced by parents at transition times. Involving and consulting with them gives them some control in the situation so they are less likely to transmit their anxiety to their children. Supportive practitioners recognise and empathise with their concerns, acknowledging their individual ways of dealing with the process and providing help and reassurance when needed.

There are strong links between transitions

This is about gathering and sharing information in the first instance, but is also about fostering and building 'professional friendships' between the different settings or 'microsystems' as described by Bronfenbrenner (1979). This includes links between home and the setting as well as between the various settings a child might experience horizontally in one day, or vertically across the years of early childhood. There must be mutual respect for the professionalism of other carers and a recognition of the importance of both the parents' and practitioners' role in the child's life.

Strong, supportive links help the child with the vital task of holding their important people in mind when they are apart from them. This might also play a part in supporting vulnerable attachments in the home or in a care setting.

They have an informal, relaxed start to the session

Leaving your mum or dad is extra hard when there is a roomful of people watching you, all sitting expectantly on the carpet waiting for the business of the day to begin. Relaxed starts, ideally staggered, are invaluable, as they allow the child and their parent to take their time separating and to choose what the child is ready to engage in.

Coming into an active environment with self-registration and continuous provision (as opposed to carpet-based registration routines) provides the child and parent with lots of options for handling the separation in ways that work best for them.

Their friendships are acknowledged

Australian studies of children making transitions from home to kindergarten or school have found that having friends in the same class helps children adjust to the demands of the new setting and can possibly help compensate for other factors that can make children more vulnerable during transition (Margetts 1997). So, ask parents and staff at previous settings about a child's friendships and be flexible in your approach to groupings etc. to take account of these.

They have the chance to think and talk about change

Children have immense capacity for thinking philosophically as well as about their immediate experiences. The opportunity to talk about planned changes is just as important to small children as it is to adults. They need to ask questions, to voice concerns and to incorporate ideas and feelings about change and transitions into their play, through story and drama, role play and in their 'small world' play. Although stories about 'going to playgroup' or 'starting school' have their place, they can sometimes be too specific to be able to reflect every child's experience. More powerful, perhaps, are classic stories and fairy tales that reflect human experience of change and uncertainty and explore what it feels like to find yourself in an unfamiliar place, conquering your fears and persevering through adversity!

Their setting is flexible

A flexible approach to admissions and settling procedures is more likely to address the needs of individual children and their families. Some children may appear to make a 'smooth' transition in the first instance, only becoming distressed at a later stage. Others will need lots of support right from the start while they take tiny steps to becoming relaxed and enthusiastic about the new setting. Some families will expect their child to separate readily, while others will anticipate that their child might struggle with change.

A 'one size fits all' approach to new admissions that expects children to fit in with existing timetables and procedures really doesn't work for anybody. Watchful and attentive practitioners in settings with a flexible approach are ready to respond to the variable needs of individual children and families and are equipped with lots of strategies to match those needs.

There is a degree of predictability

We know that uncertainty can induce stress in some children and adults. A degree of predictability can help with this, but doesn't have to mean strict adherence to a rigid timetable. The best sort of predictability gives children the certainty that there won't be too many interruptions to their sustained play, or too many breaks for adult-driven tasks, such as snack times, assemblies and whole-class discussions.

Julie Fisher considers the effect of this in her book *Moving on to Key Stage 1: Improving transition from the Early Years Foundation Stage*, and validates the importance of maintaining young children's natural momentum throughout the course of the day by not allowing school timetables to dictate and interrupt. For example, predictability for a young child is not about always having a snack at 10.30am every morning. It is much more about knowing that 'snack' is always available and in the same place every day so that they can help themselves 'when their own learning momentum is ebbing – and be refueled ready for another burst' (Fisher 2010:169).

They are encouraged to be independent

Children moving from one stage to the next can benefit from being able to rehearse new skills in the familiar setting and then gradually trying them out in the new one. Those children who lack experience or confidence in their physical independence, however, need to know that there will always be someone to help them with the tricky things that they can't do for themselves yet.

Just as important is the opportunity to develop, and maintain, high levels of intellectual independence. Young children are highly motivated to make sense of their world and their experiences, and this contributes to their valuable sense of being in control. We know that removing this sense of control can trigger stress. Sadly, all too often children are denied the opportunity to take control over what is happening to them during transitions. This is particularly relevant for children moving from the Foundation Stage into Key Stage 1, where their high levels of intellectual autonomy are sometimes not acknowledged or even appreciated. This ultimately disrupts achievement and damages positive dispositions for learning. It reduces children from independent learners working appropriately at their own developmental level to a 'whole-class' group of Y1 children waiting for the teacher to tell them what to do next!

There is a safe place to take risks and make mistakes

All children are entitled to a supportive learning environment that allows them to develop independence and self-reliance by encouraging them to try things out, take risks and comfortably learn from their mistakes. This kind of environment is constantly providing them with the skills and emotional resilience they will need to handle transition well.

For all of the above to be in place, transition must be viewed as a process, not an event

Talking with practitioners about transitions highlights the fact that the term has become, in many cases, a shorthand for all the organisational aspects of transferring a group of children from one stage to the next. Once the decisions have been made about who is going where and when, dates have been set for parents' information meetings, records and profiles have been handed over, etc., there is a sense that transitions have been 'taken care of'. Indeed, given that sometimes in the past, some of these essential organisational aspects didn't get done at all or were left to the last minute, we have to acknowledge why increased efficiency might be seen as progress! But if we take account of everything we know about young children, then it's clear that we have to view – and plan for – transition as a process and not just a tick-list of events.

Describing the process of a child's transition to autonomy and independence from the mother, the psychoanalyst Donald Winnicott writes of the trick of the 'good enough' mother giving the child a sense of 'loosening' from her rather than the shock of being 'dropped' (Winnicott 1953). This is a useful analogy for practitioners too. 'Good enough' practitioners need to hold a child through the process of transition, so that the ties from one stage are gradually loosened, allowing the child to freely explore the next stage while still feeling connected to what has gone before. Being emotionally and physically 'dropped' from the baby room into the 'two to threes room' or from nursery into reception is potentially shocking to a young child's brain and is simply never 'good enough'.

When transition is understood as a process, there is a greater likelihood that flexible policies will be created that support everyone involved to make the experience 'good enough' for every child.

The role of the practitioner in supporting transitions

The practitioners and in particular, the key people working with a child are fundamental to the success of any transition. Children experiencing transition need the following.

- **Practitioners who give them time** – to become familiar with the idea of moving on, to talk about it, to reflect on what they already know and have learned, to absorb new information, to revisit and remember what went before, to adjust to the changes and to make mistakes without the fear of being judged. Practitioners who are good at supporting transitions know that children need to be allowed time for regression as much as consolidation.

- **Practitioners who listen to them** – to find out what worries or excites them about a move, how they might like to influence aspects of the experience, and when they are telling us they need help with the little things as well as the big things. Practitioners who are active listeners acknowledge children's feelings and don't try to dismiss them as not being valid. As Julie Fisher writes, 'These after all are the people who are actually experiencing the change, so we should never make assumptions about how they are feeling about it' (Fisher 2006:10).

- **Practitioners who recognise the importance of attachment and emotional well-being** – and are able to tune into the needs of an individual child and their family in this respect. They know that children need to be sure they will receive unconditional care regardless of whether or not they or their family conform to the norms expected of them. This is not about judging the quality of attachment between parent and child, but about having the insight to recognise levels of insecurity and respond sensitively to the way that the family handles transition and separation.

- **Practitioners who offer proactive support to all** – including those who may appear to be 'coping', and don't wait for a crisis to occur before they respond. Children need practitioners who know that there is often a 'honeymoon period' for children settling in, and that some children will have less obvious ways of showing their distress and anxiety during transition and separation.

- **Practitioners who show respect for a child's way of making it work for themselves** – by listening to the child and their family about how they want to handle the separation from each other and who then adapt settling procedures to make the most of this. Practitioners who understand transition know that children often need transitional objects or particular rituals and routines to comfort themselves until they are ready to go it alone.

- **Practitioners who appreciate what the child brings with them and has learned at home or in a previous setting** – they know that this is important for the child's self-esteem as much as to set starting points for future learning, and they are not judgemental or obsessed with 'correctness', particularly with regard to physical or self-help skills. They actively seek to make and maintain strong links with home and other settings that the child has attended. They make sure they gather, read and take notice of all the information passed to them by parents and previous settings about the child's motivations and interests as well as their home culture, language, etc.

- **Practitioners who build warm, friendly links with their parents and families** – children in transition need to see that the relationship between home and the setting is strong and supportive. This is reassuring for the child and strengthens continuity between the different worlds or 'microsystems' (Bronfenbrenner 1979) experienced by the child. Much of this work begins at the 'getting to know you' stage when the child is accompanied by their parent at informal 'drop-in' sessions and in the early stages of settling. Children are able to observe their parent(s) 'making friends' with their carers, just as they are doing throughout the process.

- **Practitioners who plan carefully for transition** – they know that transitions are important and significant in a child's life and plan carefully to support them. They know that 'one size' doesn't fit all and that some children will be more vulnerable than others at times of change, so their planning is responsive rather than rigid.

- **Practitioners who are creative in their approach to supporting transition** – who challenge unnecessary moves and are open to finding innovative ways to better meet the needs of children and their families. They are flexible and adaptable in their approach and are keen to engage everyone in the process, rather than assuming that they are the only ones who know how to do it best.

- **Practitioners who are empathetic and can relate to children's anxieties and concerns around transition** – they have the skills and ability to reflect on the environment and experiences they provide for children and families and gauge how appropriate they are to the individual. They are also able to handle their own feelings triggered by a child's distress or anguish during separation and seek out help when necessary. They don't attempt to dismiss or distract a child (or parent) from their feelings and emotions during times of transition, but they acknowledge, honour and accept their sadness or anxiety as a natural and authentic response to separation. By identifying and labelling these feelings they are also helping to build an emotional vocabulary for the child and modelling empathy, demonstrating to the child that it is possible to interpret our own feelings and those of others (Fonagy 2003, cited in Gerhardt 2004:25).

The importance of home visiting

Some people have concerns that home visits can be intrusive and used to form judgements about families and their home life, so it is very important to make it clear to parents that they are under no obligation to accept a home visit, and that the purpose of the visit is not to inspect their home. My experience of home visiting has been overwhelmingly positive, and every parent who was initially anxious about a visit (especially with a first child) commented positively about the experience afterwards – and was enthusiastic about subsequent home visits for younger children.

For many communities, the opportunity to welcome practitioners into their home is embraced with enthusiasm and will involve meeting not just the child and immediate family, but grandparents and aunties and uncles too. This is so valuable for everyone concerned, not least the child, who knows that you can now help them 'hold in mind' these very special people while they are away from them. Hearing a child joyfully announce 'You came round my house!' on their first day at nursery is powerful evidence of the significance of home visiting in supporting a child's transition. However, to make the most of these precious opportunities for connecting with a child and their family on their home ground, they must be handled with sensitivity and thoughtfulness. Remember too that you may need to visit a child at their childminder's as well as their family home.

It is helpful to bear the following in mind when setting up and carrying out home visits

Guarantee parents' privacy

Offer them a home visit, rather than just sending a formal letter announcing your intention to descend upon them. Respect their wishes if they decline, and invite them instead to come to the setting for an informal meeting where you can chat and share information. Then offer a follow-up visit at a later stage when they feel more relaxed about the process.

Children often want to show you around their house, particularly their bedroom or where their toys are kept. Check first with the parents that they are comfortable with this and thank them for allowing you the privilege to connect with the child in this way.

Ensure practitioners' safety

It is important to carry out visits in pairs. Impress on managers and head teachers the value of home visits to ensure that they allocate the staff and the time needed to carry out the visits. Ensure that at least one key person takes part in the visit and is available to greet the child and their family on their first arrival in the setting.

It is also important to make sure that younger or inexperienced members of staff are well supported in home visiting. Not only does it demand a degree of self-confidence and social skill, it can also be unsettling when practitioners find themselves in home situations and cultures that are outside their experience. They may need support to feel comfortable and to remain open-minded and non-judgemental in their approach.

Gather useful and essential information

This will depend on local authority guidelines for information as well as individual requirements from settings. It is easier for parents to find information such as doctor's phone numbers while at home and helpful, and speedier, if you tell them in advance the information that you will need. It is particularly important to have accurate knowledge of a child's home language experiences. It is not enough to make assumptions about this and other important individual characteristics. We need to be knowledgeable about a child's ethnicity, language and dialect, community and locality so that we can aim to offer them some familiar sights, sounds and experiences that will help them settle.

Make sure you correctly record the names of the child and their families. Find out how the parent(s) like to be addressed and what abbreviations or pet names for their child (if any) they are happy for you to use. Ask for help pronouncing names that are unfamiliar to you and practise until you can say them perfectly.

Discuss the setting

Talk about your routines, procedures and approach, perhaps giving examples of the kinds of play experiences you provide and how these will support their child's physical, intellectual, social and emotional development.

Emphasise the importance of play in learning in the early years. Give parents the opportunity to voice any concerns they may have about their child's well-being and their transition into the setting.

Discuss the child's development without being judgemental

Encourage them to tell you about their child's progress and development and reassure them that children's development varies greatly in the early years. Find out what the child enjoys doing, how they respond to change and challenge, what is likely to upset them and what strategies have worked well for the parents (and other carers) when the child is distressed or behaves in challenging ways.

Let one practitioner focus on the parent and the other on the child

This is important, as it gives the child an important message about your interest in them, as well as allowing the parents some space to concentrate on the conversation. Bring along a book or toy to share with the child, which you can leave with them to return to the setting when they arrive. If the child wants to show you their bedroom or garden – and the family don't mind – then make the most of this valuable opportunity for the child to take the lead in the interaction. This can also be a good time to introduce any item that has the setting/school logo, such as a book bag or sweatshirt, so that the child can begin to identify themselves as a member of the group.

Prepare a welcome pack

Invite existing parents in your setting to help you produce a welcome and information pack, as they are more likely to have a good grasp of the issues that will probably concern new parents. Perhaps they might like to make a 'question and answer booklet' drawing on the questions commonly asked by parents. Or help them to create a short DVD film of the setting shot from a child's perspective. Have a photo album of images from the film available for families without a TV or DVD player. Talk through the film or album on the visit. Leave a copy with the family which they can return later when the child is settled. Include some footage of children in the setting singing a well-known song or nursery rhyme, which the child and their family can join in with at home. In addition, make a personalised little booklet for the child with photos and information about their key people.

Have an interpreter where necessary

For parents whose first language is not English, check whether or not an interpreter may be useful. Don't automatically assume it will (or will not) be required. If it is, see if there may be someone within the family who can be at home to help.

Ensure you have plenty of time

Be careful to allocate enough time for each visit so that you can really listen and engage with the parents and family members as they tell you about the child and share with you their hopes and concerns for them. Don't forget that for many families the visit may be seen as an important social occasion – this is worth remembering when offered your sixth cup of tea for the day!

Have ready some prompts for discussion

These could include:

- important adults in the child's life
- child (and family) interests
- major events in the child's life
- favourite foods/dislikes

- sleep and energy patterns
- how the child usually shows anxiety or distress
- what helps to soothe and comfort them
- the child's motivations and schema(s)
- how the parent would like to approach the separation and what they think would most help the child in their first moments apart.

Talking about these things will ultimately be more helpful (and reassuring to the parent) than ticking off a check list of assessment criteria about pencil control, number awareness or their ability to use a knife and fork.

To be able to replicate some of the routines of home, particularly for the youngest children, will be very important, so we need to know their sleep patterns and feeding routines as well as the best way to wake them or comfort and soothe them when distressed.

Hellos and goodbyes: supporting the daily transitions at the beginning and ends of sessions

In her book *Developing Attachment in Early Years Settings*, Veronica Read lists four important aspects of the role of the practitioner with regard to the parent:

- to cherish her child
- to offer unconditional acceptance
- to welcome any opportunity to work collaboratively with [the parent]
- to help support the needs of her unique child (Read 2010:55).

For the majority of parents, the time when they will need to feel most connected with and supported by practitioners will be at the beginning and end of sessions. These are sometimes referred to as 'handovers', though I'm not sure that's the best way to describe this intensely meaningful and crucial time.

The manner in which parent and child are received at the start of the day will inevitably play a big part in reassuring the parent that their child is indeed cherished. We all know that to be greeted warmly, with a welcoming smile and a caring touch, makes all the difference to the start of anyone's day. How much more important, then, if you are a small person (or an anxious parent) dealing with the transition from home and all its familiar sights, sounds and smells to this different place with its noise and hubbub and completely different sensory experiences.

A particular benefit of the key person approach is the opportunity it affords to provide a personalised start to the session. The skill of the key person lies in the way that they are able to greet each of their key children with a comment and physical connection that shows how well they hold the child (and parent) in mind. They are also able to help the parent establish loving rituals that help the separation – and reconnection – process. Becky A. Bailey's book of *I Love You Rituals* (2000) provides a useful rationale for developing little affectionate rituals that promote attachment with parents and carers and some good ideas for things to do at 'hello and goodbye' times.

Margot Sunderland points out that 'separation hurts small humans in much the same way as a physical pain' (Sunderland 2006) and that adults tend not to give as much credence to a child's emotional pain as they do to a scraped knee or bumped head.

A child who cries when separating from their parent is just doing what they are supposed to do – separation distress in young children is natural and instinctive – and it's also instinctive for the parent. What they both need at handover transition times is the soothing presence of a sensitive practitioner who understands and empathises with them and doesn't try to dismiss their anxiety or briskly 'fix' the child's distress. If we acknowledge, honour and accept how they are feeling in that moment, we not only support them through the immediate transition process, but also contribute to their long-term emotional health by not denying or attempting to repress their strong emotions.

Feeling listened to and 'understood' in this way is soothing in itself, and is often all that is needed for the child to then allow the adult to help them regulate. In particular, this can make all the difference to a child who appears to be inconsolable and where all the conventional 'distraction' strategies have failed. Apologise to them for not having understood how anxious/angry/scared they are and lovingly and unconditionally hold them through their distress, proving to them that you are comfortable with their strong emotions and able to help the child regulate them when they are ready.

Reuniting can sometimes be just as problematic and unsettling as separation. As well as being tired and possibly hungry, a child can be unsettled by the transition of leaving the socially and intellectually stimulating environment of the setting. Seeing their parent again can also remind them of how much they missed them. Parents too can be anxious about the mood their child will be in as well as the list of jobs they have to do when they get home. Think carefully about how you organise the beginnings and ends of sessions so that everyone (including the practitioners) can be as relaxed as possible, and don't forget that some children may be leaving one setting to go to the next (e.g. being picked up a by a childminder), with all the extra stress that might entail.

Supporting children with extreme attachment issues

Children who display the kinds of behaviours associated with disorganised attachment need the utmost in sensitive and responsive care and from a range of agencies and professionals. This is particularly so at times of transition. Sadly, their needs may go unrecognised at first, even though the behaviours may be extreme. These children are communicating their extreme distress (and often trauma) through their behaviour as it is the only way they have of showing us their intolerable stress.

Children presenting with challenging behaviour of any kind are often mis-understood in the first instance, because of the expectation that firm boundaries and positive disciplinary systems of reward, sanctions and consequences are all that are required to bring them into line and improve their behaviour. When that doesn't work, and by the time specialist external advice is sought, it can be too late to create the right kind of environment to support these vulnerable children.

Adopted children, as well as those still in the care system, are particularly at risk of being insecurely attached – their difficulties and needs don't go away overnight just because they have been removed from unsafe situations. The disruptions and change they have already experienced will have been very traumatic – and of all children, they particularly need consistency and reliability around them even though, paradoxically, they may well resist it. Adults behaving consistently and reliably around them may initially feel so unfamiliar to them that they are likely to feel threatened by the very thing that they need most.

These children will be particularly sensitive to all kinds of relatively minor changes throughout the day as well as more major transitions, and are likely to react with conventional inappropriate behaviour as well as in more bizarre ways. Watch out for children who begin to 'play up' or become unresponsive just before a change in routine (e.g. lunch time, break time, assembly, moving to a different room) or who cannot cope with the absence of a key person or change in teacher. Look beyond the immediate behaviour and think about how a change or transition (no matter how small or seemingly inconsequential) might have triggered threatening feelings for them. Examine the structure of the day from the child's perspective and challenge yourself to reduce as far as possible the transitions the child finds most troubling. Where change throughout the day is inevitable, think about how you support the child in advance of it, as well as during and after.

•

A developmentally appropriate curriculum

In *Moving on to Key Stage 1*, Julie Fisher provides sound advice and a range of useful strategies for supporting the transition between the EYFS and Key Stage 1. She reminds us that, in developmental terms, there is very little difference between a Foundation Stage child and a child in a Year 1 class.

> All of the child development literature that concerns children of this age says that the key changes in children's development come around the end of year 2 when children approach the age of 7. Nowhere in the literature does it say that suddenly at age 6 children prefer to learn by listening to the teacher. Nowhere does it say that children learn best when they are sitting on a carpet. Nowhere does it say that children no longer need play and no longer like learning out of doors.

> (Fisher 2010:17)

The same essential fact is true at any age. The child is fundamentally the same whether they are playing in the 'baby room' or in the 'two or threes', and their curriculum needs do not automatically change overnight on their birthday or over the course of a holiday break. A developmentally appropriate curriculum fits around the child, meeting them where they 'are at', rather than some notion of where they 'should be' – and therefore supports a smoother transition. Given that successive governments seem determined to formalise a curriculum for the early years without paying too much attention to research and scientific information about child development and pedagogy, it becomes even more important that we continue to fight for developmentally appropriate practice that goes beyond any rudimentary framework.

The work of the Campaign for Learning (www.campaign-for-learning.org.uk) and its development of the '5Rs for Lifelong Learning' provide a useful perspective that is as relevant in the early years as it is at any stage. The 5Rs are aspects of learning that are clearly relevant in supporting children to develop the self-awareness that will support them through transitions.

- *Readiness* – feeling ready, willing and able to embrace changes and make the most of them.
- *Reflectiveness* – being self-aware and curious about what has been learned in one situation and how it applies to a new situation.
- *Resourcefulness* – having the skills and attitudes to experiment, take risks and find their own solutions to new problems.
- *Responsibility* – feeling in control of new situations, having empathy for others struggling with change and offering support.
- *Resilience* – feeling secure enough in one's self-identity to manage difficult feelings and keep going in challenging situations (www.campaignforlearning. org.uk/cfl/learninginschools/l2l/5rs.asp; accessed 28 May 2011).

REFLECTION TASK

Have a think about . . . how the 5Rs can support transition

- Have you observed young children who exemplify these aspects?
- What do the 5Rs look like in an early years setting?
- What kinds of playful experience and activity help children develop the 5Rs?
- What is our role in supporting children to develop them?
- Can you see the relevance of the 5Rs in your own learning and development?

Supporting attachment and continuity through play and playfulness

Play is a bridge that should link all elements of the EYFS experience together for babies and young children. From the youngest of babies to the relative maturity of a child in Y1, the opportunity to play and be playful is an entitlement that should be in evidence whether they are being cared for in their own home, with a childminder, in a nursery or at school. Continuity should be there in the resources and materials for them to play with and in the playful responses of the adults working with them.

Many years ago, I worked in an infant and nursery school that for a time had a home liaison nursery teacher who made weekly visits to children prior to their start at nursery. She was a familiar sight in the local streets, with her shopping trolley full of toys that she took to each home. She was not only providing a valuable and familiar link between home and the nursery, she was also supporting parents at home to understand the value of play and playfulness and her presence made a considerable difference to the transition experience for those children.

The importance of friendships

Bronfenbrenner (1979; see Chapter 3) reminds us of the importance of having a familiar person to support us through transition. The parent or key person has an obvious importance here, but children's friendships are also very relevant. Empathy, self-awareness and resilience are important in the development of good social skills and are, in turn, supported and extended by high-quality, playful, social experiences. Observe children's friendship choices and recognise where peer support may be useful in helping them handle daily transitions as well more major change.

Parents too benefit from peer support and for some, the social contact and connections made through their child's early years are of major significance. Find ways to enable parents to support each other, particularly at times of transition, by providing opportunities for socialising and connecting. Simple things like providing comfortable and relaxing spaces where parents gather at the beginning and end of sessions can be most valuable in promoting social contact as well as the provision of more formal parent meetings and workshops.

Transitional objects

Veronica Read discusses this important aspect of transition support, describing how Donald Winnicott, the psychoanalyst, explains what is happening for the child who keeps close to them a bit of blanket, soft toy or other favoured object.

> The baby, he says, is exploring a potential space, a 'me' and 'not me' space, as a solution to experiencing the beginnings of what will be later separateness.

The 'snuggly' is the baby's creative response to this new experience. The object signifies a part of the 'not me' world yet is a reminder of mother. The tactile, soft object with the smell of the mother is used as if it is the mother.

(Read 2010:62)

Winnicott was describing more than just the transition of the child being apart from the mother in the physical sense of being in a different location. It is about the much more fundamental growing awareness, on the part of the child, that they are indeed separate from the mother and a person in their own right. However, this is still relevant in terms of the child experiencing a transition into care outside the home, and most parents and practitioners are well aware of the power of such objects. Maria Robinson also talks about the importance of 'comforters' as 'things that helps babies in the transition between external comforting and "internalizing" the comforting feeling. The baby is learning to self-soothe and self-regulate their distressed feelings' (Robinson 2003:109) and for some children these objects continue to play an important role long after babyhood.

This can sometimes be seen as inconvenient when a child reaches the classroom still needing an actual 'security blanket', although by this stage it may be any object of the moment that they urgently need to bring with them from home. Understanding and appreciating the role that comforters play helps us to respond sensitively to their presence and prevents inappropriate policing of the 'anything brought from home has to go in the cupboard' variety. If it's important to the child's security then it needs to be somewhere it can be seen – and touched and sniffed and held – until it's no longer required. For some children a memento is what is required – a photo, a hanky with a parent's scent, a scarf or little keepsake. Other's benefit from a 'virtual' transitional object – a kiss or a smile to keep in their pocket, for when it's needed, or an imaginary 'heart string' that stretches from the parent to the child and can't be broken even though it stretches all the way from home to the classroom! Help parents explore the ways that they can make use of these powerful images to strengthen connection and support their child with separation.

Feeling 'at home'

We want the children we care for to 'feel at home' with us, because we know that in an ideal world, 'home' is the best place for feeling safe, relaxed and nurtured. Margaret McMillan believed the nursery school should be like an extension of home (Bruce et al. 2010:445). If we draw on Bourdieu's idea of *habitus* (see Chapter 4) then it is important that we reflect on the ways that the *habitus* of a setting might differ from the *habitus* of the child at home, and how this might affect the child in transition. The more we know of a child's home experiences, the more we can aim to reflect positive elements of that in the setting. However, we have to be realistic – it just isn't possible to reflect every element of every child's home experience. So perhaps we need to focus just as much on the emotional experience of feeling 'at home' and work to replicate that for every child.

This was brought home to me when I was co-ordinator of an integrated early years unit in a primary school. We had working with us for a short time an educational adviser from Bangladesh. He was there specifically to learn about the provision for early years children in the UK so that it could be replicated back in his home city. He spent two weeks with us and on his final day he commented that the biggest surprise for him was how much our setting was like a 'home' rather than the school setting he had been expecting. He recognised this as much in the attitudes and nurturing care displayed by the practitioners as in the way the rooms were laid out. He believed this subtle difference was also reflected in the happy and relaxed attitudes of children and staff, which he acknowledged also contributed to the children's motivations and enthusiasm for learning.

The key person approach is an important element of the way in which we create settings that are 'best understood as an extension of home, where children meet a wider range of adults and children but are still mainly cared for by a small number of people, in relationships that replicate some aspects of home relationships' (Elfer et al. 2012:6). An atmosphere of reciprocal warmth and nurture is beneficial for practitioners and parents too, who also need to feel 'at home' in the environment for the best results for everyone.

Professional love

If we are aiming to create settings that replicate the warmth of a loving home, then we must also take seriously the concept of 'professional love' and the part it plays in supporting transitions.

As Maria Robinson writes, 'Loving is also about nurture, and what professionals who work with infants and their families actually do is nurture them, providing a secure base away from the home or encouraging security within the child's home' (Robinson 2003:158). Jools Page writes extensively about this in *Working with Babies and Children from Birth to Three*, and suggests that 'the work of early childhood professionals involves not only "care and education" but "*love*, care and education"' (Page and Nutbrown 2008:183; emphasis in original). She goes on to state the case for an honest and open exploration of the importance of 'professional love' in the framework for early years qualifications and policy-making 'alongside and with as much importance as "leadership and management", "cognitive development" and "phonics". Let's start talking about loving babies and young children' (Page and Nutbrown 2008:187).

If we are concerned about the impact of early transitions on our youngest children, then we have to reaffirm the importance of this complex and challenging thing called 'professional love' and its fundamental role at the heart of the key person approach.

Being an 'emotionally aware caregiver'

Margot Sunderland and others are clear in their advice to parents that if they need to leave their young child in the care of another they must establish first that they are an 'emotionally aware care-giver' (Sunderland 2006:57). In turn, this acknowledges the great responsibility that carers, practitioners and teachers carry – it is our job to become a secondary attachment figure for the children we work with and this demands a degree of emotional awareness we don't always get the credit for. Understanding attachment theory and early brain development is part of this responsibility, as it helps us to recognise what individual children need to help them, not just in the separation process but throughout their time with us.

Veronica Read is very clear about the inappropriateness of labelling and categorising attachment styles in children, but also provides us with some helpful insights as to how best to support children's attachments. We can use what we know about the different behaviours that are linked with different styles of attachment to tune into what individual children might need, particularly at times of transition. She suggests that 'Children who come into Early Years settings who are securely attached need to continue to experience an optimum level of support and nurturing care – this is best achieved amongst other things through the key person approach' (Read 2010:36).

Children who are showing the types of behaviour associated with insecure avoidant attachment need 'help building relationships and by offering reassurance on a daily basis they may develop enough trust to risk seeking care, and begin to

---

REFLECTION TASK

Have a think about . . .

. . . how you evaluate the transition process for individual children:

- How do you recognise when a child feels like 'a fish in water' in your setting?
- What tells you that they feel 'held in mind' by the people who are important to them?
- How do they show you that they have a sense of belonging?
- What are the indicators that a child is 'ready, willing and able' to make the most of their new situation?

. . . how you evaluate the transition process for parents and families:

- Once their child is well settled, ask parents for their feedback on the process (Lindon 2010).
- Find out what worked for them and what they might have wanted to do differently.

believe their needs will be understood and they will not be rejected' (Read 2010:36).

Children displaying insecure ambivalent attachment behaviour are best helped by 'confident, consistent and predictable care, with warnings about unexpected changes and certainty that the adult is holding them "in mind", thus leaving them calm and secure enough to explore the external world' (Read 2010:36).

The importance of observation

Observation is fundamental to our evaluation of children's well-being during transition and will probably feature prominently in your answers to the task on p. 118. Think about the process and systems you have in place to observe, analyse and make sense of the vital information that children provide through their actions, communication and general behaviours during times of change and transition. Settling diaries are a good idea – you can record timings and lengths of stay etc. as well as the child's responses and successful strategies for dealing with distress and upset. These can be helpful in deciding next steps in settling with parents, and useful for informing plans for future transitions for individuals.

Use the questions in the task box as starting points for observation to gauge just how well a child really is settling – rather than just coping – with transition.

Learning journeys

One way to provide a thread of continuity through the various transitions experienced is through the continuous formal recording of a child's learning journey. As an example, staff at a Children's Centre were able to draw together the various strands of a child's experience with them in

- the crèches and family groups provided by the centre
- the daycare provision in the on-site private nursery
- the primary school reception class also on their premises.

They looked carefully at how they could co-create learning journeys that accompanied the child throughout their time in the EYFS. Establishing this system involved discussion around training for practitioners as well as issues around suitable formats, storage and how best to share the process with parents. Done well, these documents not only will provide a fascinating and joyful celebration of the children's experiences during their early years, they will also provide meaningful information on a child's progress for parents and practitioners along the way – and for Y1 staff when children finally leave the EYFS.

Endings, as well as beginnings

However we may feel about the multiple transitions to which young children are exposed in their early years, there still exists a desire to mark and celebrate the significance of leaving nursery and starting school. We must beware of imposing our adult perspectives on this in our eagerness to commemorate the 'graduation' from one setting to another. A celebration of the children's achievements and special ways of marking the occasion are one thing, but we have to acknowledge that the increasing tendency to market it with commercially produced gowns, mortarboards and beribboned certificates is perhaps more for the benefit of the adults than for the children. It is the personal and individual ways that carers honour and celebrate their 'leavers' that is most likely to support the child with the process, enabling them to feel positive not just about themselves but also about the changes to come.

Saying goodbye to children and families we have worked with over a period of time can be emotional for practitioners too. It is heartening to see children grow and thrive and to assess just how far they have come since we first knew them. But for key people in particular, it can be a wrench to see them go. Elfer and colleagues pose this important question about the ending of the key person relationship, either as the child leaves the EYFS or when they transfer to a new key person within the setting: 'How will you let go of the special professional intimacy of your attachment to your key children when they move on? This work of ending is as important as the work of preparing and establishing the special relationship at the beginning' (Elfer et al. 2012:117).

Mentoring and 'supervision' for key people can be essential at this stage to ensure that professional boundaries are maintained and also to support practitioners in acknowledging and celebrating 'the special part you played as a Key Person in the child's well-being, positive self identity, mental health, learning and friendships in their formative early years' (Elfer et al. 2012:117).

Thinking creatively about transition

Be creative in your approach to transitions and challenge yourself to look at your practice from the perspective of individual children and their families. This transition audit (O'Connor 2006) summarises the key points from this chapter. Use it to help with a review of your practice and to evaluate your setting's transition policies.

In all transitions

Do you:

- meet with senior management and all relevant staff well in advance to discuss and evaluate policies for transition and settling? Does management give special consideration to times of transition (for children, parents and staff) and ensure that staff have enough time to prepare?

- organise and support a full home visiting programme?

- allocate sufficient time for staff to access, read and share information?

- plan a programme of frequent drop-in sessions as well as formal visits?

- share transition plans with parents (and children, where relevant)?

- evaluate correspondence to parents? Is the tone welcoming, the information direct? Does it invite parents to become involved in the process and suggest ways they can help you to help their child?

- allow children time for the settling process, to regress a little, to stand and watch others until they are ready to join in, to keep their parent, carer or transitional object with them as long as they need?

- look at ways to support and develop children's friendships and 'buddy systems' that provide encouragement and security in new situations? Think about how this might work for parents also. Help them to make links with each other for support and advice.

- respond sensitively to parent anxieties? Are you aware of why some parents are overanxious (for example, their child is first or last born, or has health problems, or the family has domestic difficulties)? Are you supportive, but firm, with parents who put their own needs first (due to, for example, work commitments) when it comes to the settling process?

- plan how to support and enable parents settling their children? Do you offer flexibility at the start of sessions so that parents stay as long as they need, a place for them to go when they first leave their children for a short while, opportunities for them to meet and chat with other parents going through the same experience?

- keep a record of children's transition process, noting length and timing of stay and the reasons for reducing or extending the process?

- observe children during periods of transition, monitoring their emotional well-being, their coping strategies and any indicators of stress?

- record significant achievements and signs that the child is settling in and starting to feel safe and secure in the new environment? Do you record children's thoughts and opinions about planned moves and anticipated transitions, noting their anxieties and concerns as well as motivation and excitement about change and 'moving on'?

Between home and setting

Do you:

- offer home visits?
- plan a timetable for home visits, including interpreters and key people?
- prepare welcome packs?
- develop an admission form/home visiting format that allows parents to tell you everything they want you to know about their child?
- use this information to plan the learning environment (for example, responding to children's interests and schemas)?
- use photographs of the child and their family (taken with parental permission) for labels and in welcoming displays?
- offer staggered admissions so that children and staff aren't overwhelmed?
- ask older/outgoing children to share their thoughts on the transition process from when they arrived in the setting?
- encourage them to prepare materials and information that they think will be helpful to new children?
- offer flexible/staggered start times and individual settling programmes?
- access and read all incoming information on individual children, and highlight those likely to be vulnerable or less resilient and have special or additional needs?
- brief all relevant staff on information that will help them support not just the child but also their key carers in helping the child to settle?
- review each child's settling on a daily basis with parents and key carers?

Internally within the same setting

As well as the above, do you:

- ensure that relevant information about the child and their family is regularly updated and current even if everyone feels they 'already know' the child and family, based on earlier information?
- provide time for children to visit the new room informally, with a key person?
- plan individual transitions flexibly so that children make the move when they are ready, rather than because of a birthday or gap in numbers?
- plan to move children in friendship groups together or in pairs, so that they don't have to experience transition alone?
- plan for new key people to spend time with the child in their current room and to receive all relevant information from current carers?
- allow children the opportunity to revisit their previous rooms and key people?

- provide opportunities for children to explore their experience of change and 'moving on' through role play, story and drama, small world play, etc.?

- provide mentoring and support for key people so that they can form strong positive relationships with their children and provide meaningful assessments of their children to inform new carers?

- regularly review organisation and groupings to consider ways to remove or reduce transitions within the setting?

Between EYFS settings (including school reception classes)

As well as the above, do you:

- visit and observe children in their previous setting(s), noting significant routines, and learning approaches?

- provide as much information as possible about your setting?

- ensure that children will still have constant access to outdoors and resources necessary for all the areas of learning in the EYFS curriculum?

- where possible, use a staff member as a 'bridging person' who moves between the settings to support children with the move?

- talk with parents about the EYFS curriculum and how you plan for children's progress across settings?

Between EYFS and Year 1

As well as the above, do you provide opportunities:

- for parents and children to know well in advance their likely new teachers and classrooms?

- for children and parents to visit Year 1 classrooms and relevant staff well in advance of the move?

- for Year 1 staff to spend time observing children at play, the organisation and routines of EYFS classes and the ways that EYFS staff support child-initiated activities?

- for EYFS practitioners to share EYFS stage assessment profiles and learning journeys with Year 1 staff, and explain how these help establish starting points for each child?

- for children to raise questions, talk about their concerns, and have these feelings acknowledged?

- for children to reflect upon and share their achievements with Year 1 staff as well as their current practitioners?

- for children to talk about how they would like to handle the move and incorporate their suggestions?

■ for children to devise their own ways to commemorate their 'graduation' from the Foundation Stage to Y1, acknowledging their progress and achievements, e.g. with a party, assembly or souvenir scrapbook?

As Year 1 staff, do you also:

■ familiarise yourself with the EYFS curriculum guidance and books and materials supporting transition into Key Stage 1?

■ read EYFS assessments and records on each child ahead of their arrival and discuss them with EYFS staff?

■ discuss ways to make the most of the learning that has already taken place and identify children who are talented or gifted, have additional needs and may initially continue to need a modified EYFS curriculum (such as children who are summer born, very active or have had a disadvantaged time at Foundation Stage)?

■ invite parents to an informal session soon after the move so the children can show off their new class and teacher?

The time and effort put into thinking about transition, creating flexible transition policies, and ensuring that children's voices are heard in the process will be well worth it in the long term.

Conclusion

But change is just a part of life isn't it? The children seem to cope OK – it's how they learn to get used to it.

I have heard a version of this statement many times as I've tried to explain why I'm writing about transitions. Change is fundamental to life and always has been – the rituals and rites of passage from childhood into adulthood, the readjustment that comes with new life and death, the circumstances that dictate a move from one house to another and further afield. And transition, where one moves from one stage to the next, is part of the process.

Transition can be transforming, as the person who existed in one setting, stage or place moves on and becomes the person who exists in, and relates to, the next one. It can trigger progress if the environment the person moves into is exactly what they need at that time in their life and they feel ready to embrace the new challenge and experiences presented to them. But if they are not feeling ready and the environment isn't the right one for them at that time, then the experience will be challenging and might stall progress altogether.

The amount of research material and books written on transition relating to children – and particularly children starting school – would suggest that this is a real cause for concern. Babies and young children are experiencing more transitions in their first five or six years of life than is good for them. Some of our most vulnerable will probably experience more traumatic change in their early years than some of us do throughout our lives! As Stig Brostrom (2002) says, that should make them 'transition experts'. But evidence suggests that is not the case and that we may be creating untold damage in future generations by not paying enough attention to the need for constancy and predictability in the early years of life.

In its review of transition research literature, the Centre for Excellence in Children and Young People's Services (2010) highlights the need for further research into aspects of transition. With particular reference to the early years, it suggests that this should include studies:

- to compare the 'typical' English system of separate pre-school, primary and secondary schools with other systems that avoid transitions, such as early years units and all-age schools;

- to examine early years transitions and evaluate the longer term impact of interventions designed to prevent or reduce transition challenges;

- to evaluate the impact of the Independent Review of the Primary Curriculum (2009) and the single point of entry into school on children's experience of transition and the effect on their progress.

It also recommends that future studies should include the perspectives of children, families and staff and consider the full range of outcomes for children. It suggests that children's stress and anxiety, motivation, self-confidence and attitudes to learning should be examined as well as academic progress. This is heartening, as it suggests a growing awareness of the broader impact of transition and the particular significance of transition in the early years of life.

My own understanding of the impact of transition has been informed by my professional experience in nursery, infant and primary schools, and personal experience as an adoptive parent of a child who is at the extreme end of the spectrum in terms of negative experience of change. While I was writing this book, my now teenage son was transitioning from compulsory schooling into further education (and out of it again), and I was struck by the potential similarities of the transition experience at both ends of the school experience. There was a great deal of talk about how school and college would support transition and some exemplary practice on the part of individuals in both settings. But in reality, little attention was paid to the emotional impact of change or the need to view transition as a process – and a potentially lengthy one at that.

The same principles relating to transition apply at whatever age. But by getting it right for our youngest children and providing them with positive and appropriate transition experiences now, we build the emotional strength and resilience that will be needed to deal successfully with the inevitable changes that later life will surely bring.

> [T]he only certainty in life will be uncertainty, because the world they are inheriting, and in turn, reshaping, is characterized by change.
>
> (Brooker 2008)

References and further reading

Ahnert, L., Gunnar, M. R., Lamb, M. E., & Barthel, M. (2004). Transition to child care: Associations with infant–mother attachment, infant negative emotion, and cortisol elevation. *Child Development, 75*(3), 639–650.

Ainsworth, M., Blehar, M., Waters, E., and Wall, S. (1978). *Patterns of attachment: A psychological study of the Strange Situation.* Hillsdale, NJ: Lawrence Erlbaum Associates.

Alfvén, G. (2004). Plasma oxytocin in children with recurrent abdominal pain. *Journal of Pediatric Gastroenterology and Nutrition, 38,* 513–517.

Bailey, B. A. (2000). *I Love You Rituals.* New York, NY: HarperCollins.

Balbernie, R. (2007). *Cortisol and the early years.* Available at www.whataboutthechildren.org.uk/images/stories/PDF's/Cortisol%20and%20the%20Early%20Years.pdf (accessed 5 February 2012).

Baldock, P. (2011). *Developing early childhood services past, present and future.* Maidenhead, UK: Open University Press.

Beatson J., & Taryon, S. (2003). Predispositions to depression: The role of attachment. *Australian and New Zealand Journal of Psychiatry,* April, 219–225.

Bernstein, B. (1971). *Class, codes and control: Theoretical studies towards a sociology of language.* London, UK: Routledge and Kegan Paul.

Bilton, H. (2002). *Outdoor play in the early years: Management and innovation.* London, UK: David Fulton.

Blackledge, A. (2000). Education, diversity and social justice, *NALDIC News, 22,* November. Available at www.naldic.org.uk/Resources/NALDIC/Initial%20Teacher%20Education/Documents/KRBlackledge.pdf (accessed 7 February 2012).

Blackstone, T. (1971). *A fair start: The provision of pre-school education.* London, UK: Allen Lane.

Bombèr, L. (2007). *Inside I'm hurting.* London, UK: Worth Publishing.

Bourdieu, P., & Waquant, L. (1992). *An invitation to reflexive sociology.* Chicago, IL: University of Chicago Press.

Bowlby, J. (1969). *Attachment and loss, Vol. 1: Attachment.* New York, NY: Basic Books and Hogarth Press.

Bowlby, J. (1973). *Attachment and loss, Vol. 2: Separation: Anxiety & anger.* New York, NY: Basic Books.

Bowlby, J. (1980). *Attachment and loss, Vol. 3: Loss: Sadness & depression.* New York, NY: Basic Books.

Bowlby, J. (1988). *A secure base: Clinical applications of attachment theory.* London, UK: Routledge.

Bowlby, R. (2007). *Stress in daycare.* Available at www.whataboutthechildren.org.uk/images/stories/PDF's/The%20Need%20for%20Secondary%20Attachment%20Figures%20in%20Childcare.pdf (accessed 3 February 2012). Also on YouTube: www.youtube.com/watch?v=WPcNoGl1Lkw (accessed 13 February 2012).

Bremner, J. D., & Narayan, M. (1998). The effects of stress on memory and the hippocampus throughout the life cycle: Implications for childhood development and aging. *Developmental Psychology, 10,* 871–885.

Bronfenbrenner, U. (1979). *The ecology of human development: Experiments by nature and design.* Cambridge, MA: Harvard University Press.

Brooker, L. (2008). Supporting transitions in the early years. Maidenhead, UK: Open University Press.

Brostrom, S. (2002). Communication and continuity in the transition from kindergarten to school. In Dunlop, A. & Fabian, H. (Eds.) (2002). *Transitions in the early years: Debating continuity and progression for children in the early years.* London, UK: Routledge Falmer.

Bruce, T. (2005). *Early childhood education.* New York, NY: Oxford University Press.

Bruce, T. (2011). EYFS Best Practice: All about . . . Friedrich Froebel. *Nursery World,* 6 April.

Bruce, T., Meggitt, C., & Grenier, J. (2010). *Child care and education.* London, UK: Hodder Arnold.

Campaign for Learning (undated). *The 5 Rs of lifelong learning.* Available at www.campaignforlearning.org.uk/cfl/learninginschools/l2l/5rs.asp (accessed 6 February 2012).

Carlson, E., Daley, T., Bitterman, A., Heinzen, H., Keller, B., Markowitz, J., et al. (2009). *Early school transitions and the social behavior of children with disabilities: Selected findings from the Pre-Elementary Education Longitudinal Study: Wave 3. Overview report from the Pre-Elementary Education Longitudinal Study (PEELS).* Washington, DC: Institute of Education Sciences. Available at http://ies.ed.gov/ncser/pdf/20093016.pdf (accessed 29 May 2012).

Carr, M. (2011). *Assessment in early childhood settings: Learning stories.* London, UK: Paul Chapman Publishing.

Centre for Community Child Health (2008). *Rethinking the transition to school: Linking schools and early years services* (Policy Brief 11). Parkville, Australia: The Royal Children's Hospital, Centre for Community Child Health. Available at www.rch.org.au/emplibrary/ccch/PB11_Transition_to_school.pdf (accessed 20 January 2010).

Centre for Excellence in Children and Young People's Services (2010). *Ensuring that all children and young people make sustained progress and remain fully engaged through all transitions between key stages.* Available at www.c4eo.org.uk/themes/schools/sustainedprogress/files/sustained_progress_research_review.pdf (accessed 12 February 2012).

Cline, F. (1992). *Hope for high risk and rage-filled children.* Evergreen, CO: EC Publications.

Cline, F. (undated). *Needs, trust and personality development: The cycle of bonding and attachment.* Available at www.fostercline.com (accessed 12 February 2012).

Cozolino, L. (2006) *The neuroscience of human relationships.* London, UK: Norton.

Crawford, C., Dearden, L., & Meghir, C. (2007). *When you are born matters: The impact of date of birth on child cognitive outcomes in England.* London, UK: Institute for Fiscal Studies. Available at www.ifs.org.uk//docs/born_matters_report.pdf (accessed 28 January 2010).

Crittenden, P. M., & Claussen, A. H. (Eds.). (2000). *The organisation of attachment relationships.* Cambridge, UK: Cambridge University Press.

Department for Children, Education, Lifelong Learning and Skills (DCELLS). (2008). *Framework for children's learning for 3–7 year olds in Wales.* Cardiff, UK: Welsh Assembly.

Department for Children, Schools and Families (DCSF). (2008). *The Early Years Foundation Stage.* Nottingham, UK: DfES Publications.

Department for Education. (2009). *Independent review of the primary curriculum.* London, UK: DfE.

Department for Education and Employment (DfEE). (1997). *Excellence in schools.* White Paper. London, UK: DfEE.

Department for Education and Employment (DfEE). (1998). *Meeting the childcare challenge: A framework and consultation document.* London, UK: DfEE.

Department for Education and Employment (DfEE). (2000). *Curriculum guidance for the Foundation Stage.* London, UK: DfEE/QCA.

Department for Education and Skills (DfES). (2002). *Birth to three matters: A framework to support children in their earliest years.* London, UK: DfES/Sure Start.

Department for Education and Skills (DfES). (2004). *Effective provision of pre-school education (EPPE) project: Findings from preschool to end of Key Stage 1.* London, UK: DfES.

Department for Education and Skills (DfES). (2006). *The Early Years Foundation Stage: Consultation on a single quality framework for services to children from birth to five.* London, UK: DfES.

Dettling, A., Gunnar, M., & Donzella, B. (1999). Cortisol levels of young children in full-day childcare centres. *Psychoneuroendocrinology, 25,* 519–536.

Dettling, A., Parker, S., Lane, S., Sebanc, A., & Gunnar, M. (2000). Quality of care and temperament determine changes in cortisol concentrations over the day for young children in childcare. *Psychoneuroendocrinology, 25,* 819–836.

Devon County Council. (undated). *Early years and childcare in schools.* Available at www.devon.gov.uk/eycs-schools-fsu?nocache=8118 (accessed 6 February 2012).

Directgov. (undated). *Free early education for three and four year olds.* Available at www.direct. gov.uk/en/Parents/Preschooldevelopmentandlearning/NurseriesPlaygroupsReception Classes/DG_10013534 (accessed 9 February 2012).

Dockett, S. & Perry, B. (2007). Children's transition to school: Changing expectations. In A. Dunlop & H. Fabian (Eds.), *Informing transitions in the early years: Research, policy and practice.* Maidenhead, UK: Open University Press.

Dowling, M. (2005). *Young children's personal, social and emotional development* (2nd ed.). London, UK: Paul Chapman Publishing.

Dunlop, A., & Fabian, H. (Eds.). (2002). *Transitions in the early years: Debating continuity and progression for children in the early years.* London, UK: Routledge Falmer.

Effective Provision of Pre-School Education Project (2004). *Findings from the pre-school period.* Available at http://eppe.ioe.ac.uk/eppe/eppepdfs/RB%20summary%20findings%20from %20Preschool.pdf (accessed 14 February 2012).

Elfer, P., Goldschmied, E., & Selleck, D. Y. (2012). *Key persons in the early years: Building relationships for quality provision in early years settings and primary schools* (2nd ed.). London, UK: David Fulton.

Evangelou, M., Taggart, B., Sylva, K., Melhuish, E., & Sammons, P. (2008). *What makes a successful transition from primary to secondary school?* (Effective Pre-School, Primary and Secondary Education 3–14 Project, DCSF research report 019). London, UK: DCSF.

Evans, M. (2011). All about . . . Childminding. *Nursery World,* 9–22 August.

Fabian, H. (2002). *Children Starting School: A Guide to successful transitions and transfers for teachers and assistants.* London, UK: David Fulton.

Featherstone, S., & Bailey, R. (2006). *Smooth transitions: Ensuring continuity in the Foundation Stage.* London, UK: Featherstone Education.

Fisher, J. (2006). Handle with care! Transitions in the early years. *Early Education,* Autumn, 7–10.

Fisher, J. (2010). *Moving on to Key Stage One: Improving transition from the Early Years Foundation Stage.* Oxford, UK: Oxford University Press.

Fonagy, P. (2003). The development of psychopathology from infancy to adulthood: The mysterious unfolding of disturbance in time. *Infant Mental Health Journal, 24*(3), 212–239.

Galton, M., Gray, J., Ruddock, J. with Berry, M., Demetriou, H., Edwards, J., et al. (2003). *Transfer and transitions in the middle years of schooling (7–14): Continuities and discontinuities* (DfES Research Report 443). London, UK: DfES.

Gerhardt, S. (2004). *Why love matters: How affection shapes a baby's brain.* London, UK: Routledge.

Gerhardt, S. (2010). *The selfish society: How we all forgot to love one another and made money instead.* London, UK: Simon and Schuster.

Goldschmied, E., & Jackson, S. (1994). *People under three: Young children in daycare.* London, UK: Routledge.

Gott, S. (2009). *Teach to inspire better behaviour: Strategies for coping with aggressive, disruptive and unpredictable behaviours.* London, UK: Optimus Education.

Gunnar, M. R., & Barr, R. G. (1998). Stress, early brain development, and behaviour. *Infants & Young Children, 11*(1), 1–14.

Gunnar, M. R., & Cheatham, C. L. (2003). Brain and behaviour interface: Stress and the developing brain. *Infant Mental Health Journal, 24*(3), 195–211.

Hall, F., Hughes, D., & Jarrett, M. (2004). *Where's my peg? A parent and child guide to the first experiences of school.* London, UK: Save the Children.

Heath, S. B. (1983). *Ways with words: Language, life and work in communities and classroom.* Cambridge, UK: Cambridge University Press.

Heaton, K. (1999). *Your bowels.* London, UK: British Medical Association/Dorling Kindersley.

Heim, C., Owens, M. J., Plotsky, P. M., & Nemeroff, C. B. (1997). Persistent changes in corticotrophin-releasing factor systems due to early life stress: Relationship to the pathophysiology of major depression and post-traumatic stress disorder. *Psychopharmacology Bulletin, 33*, 185–192.

Herry, C., Bach, D. R., Esposito, F., Di Salle, F., Perrig, W. J., Scheffler, K., et al. (2007). Processing of temporal unpredictability in human and animal amygdala. *Journal of Neuroscience, 27*, 5958–5966.

House, R. (Ed.). (2011). *Too much too soon? Early learning and the erosion of childhood.* Stroud, UK: Hawthorn Press.

Jarrett, M. E., Burr, R. L, Cain, K. C., Hertig, V., Weisman, P., & Heitkemper, M. M. (2003). Anxiety and depression are related to autonomic nervous system function in women with irritable bowel syndrome. *Digestive Diseases and Sciences, 48*, 386–394.

Jennings, S. (2011). *Healthy attachments and neuro-dramatic play.* London, UK: Jessica Kingsley.

Jensen, E. (2011). *Emotions in students.* Available at www.jensenlearning.com/news/emotions-in-students/brain-based-learning (accessed 5 February 2012).

Katz, L. (1993). *Dispositions as educational goals.* Available at www.ericdigests.org/1994/goals.htm (accessed 5 February 2012).

Katz, L. (1995). *The benefits of mixed-age grouping.* Available at http://ceep.crc.uiuc.edu/eece archive/digests/1995/lkmag95.html (accessed 13 February 2012).

Ladd, C. O., Owens, M. J., & Nemeroff, C. B. (1996). Persistent changes in corticotrophin-releasing factor neuronal systems induced by maternal deprivation. *Endocrinology, 137*, 1212–1218.

Laevers, F. (Ed.) (2005). *Well-being and Involvement in care: A process-oriented self-evaluation instrument for care settings.* Available at www.kindengezin.be/img/sics-ziko-manual.pdf (accessed 6 February 2012).

Leach, P. (1978). *Your baby and child.* London, UK: Dorling Kindersley.

Lindon, J. (2010). *The key person approach: Positive relationships in the early years.* London, UK: Practical Pre-School Books.

LoCasale-Crouch, J., Mashburn, A. J., Downer, J. T., & Pianta, R. C. (2008). Pre-kindergarten teachers' use of transition practices and children's adjustment to kindergarten. *Early Childhood Research Quarterly, 23*, 124–139.

Lorenz, K. Z. (1935). Der Kumpan in der Umvelt des Vogels. *J. Orn., Berl., 83*, English translation in C. H. Schiller (Ed.), *Instinctive behaviour*. New York, NY: International Universities Press (1957).

Maclean, P. D. (1990). *The triune brain in evolution: Role of paleocerebral functions*. New York, NY: Plenum.

Margetts, K. (1997). Factors impacting on children's adjustment to the first year of primary school. *Early childhood folio 3: A collection of recent research*. Wellington, New Zealand: NZCER.

McEwen, B. S. (1999). Stress and the aging hippocampus. *Frontiers in Neuroendocrinology, 20*, 49–70.

McIntyre, L. L., Eckert, T. L., Fiese, B. H., DiGennaro, F. D., & Wildenger, L. K. (2007). Transition to kindergarten: Family experiences and involvement. *Early Childhood Education Journal, 35*, 83–88.

Merry, R. (2007). The construction of different identities within an early childhood centre: A case study in informing transitions in the early years. In A. W. Dunlop & H. Fabian (Eds.), *Informing transitions in the early years: Research, policy and practice* (pp. 45–57). Maidenhead, UK: Open University Press.

Michaels, S. (1986). Narrative presentations: An oral preparation for literacy with first-graders. In J. Cook-Gumperz (Ed.), *The social construction of literacy*. Cambridge, UK: Cambridge University Press.

Miller, A. L., Gouley, K. K., Shields, A., Dickstein, S., Seifer, R., Magee, K. D., & Fox, C. (2003). Brief functional screening for transition difficulties prior to enrolment predicts socioemotional competence and school adjustment in Head Start preschoolers. *Early Child Development and Care, 173*, 681–698.

Miller, R., & Miller, L. (2008). Key caring childminders. *Early Education Journal*, no. 55, Summer.

Nathan, C. H. (1943). Children's nurseries. *Nursery World*, 29 April, 401.

National Childminding Association. (undated). *NCMA's beliefs*. Available at www.ncma.org.uk/about_ncma.aspx (accessed 13 February 2012).

National Education Goals Panel. (1991). The National Education Goals Report. Washington, DC: National Education Goals Panel.

Niesel, R., & Greibel, W. (2007). Enhancing the competence of transition systems through co-construction. In A. Dunlop & H. Fabian (Eds.), *Informing transitions in the early years: Research, policy and practice*. Maidenhead, UK: Open University Press.

O'Connor, A., (2002). *All together now*. Available at www.nurseryworld.co.uk/news/724998/together (accessed 29 May 2012).

O'Connor, A., (2006) *All about . . . Transitions*. Available at www.schools.bedfordshire.gov.uk/early_years/Documents/Assessment%20and%20Progression/Transitions/All%2520about%2520-%2520transitions.pdf (accessed 29 May 2012).

O'Connor, A., (2007/2008). *Positive relationships: Attachment*. Available at www.nurseryworld. co.uk (accessed 29 May 2012).

Ofsted (2010). *Annual Report 2009/10*. London, UK: Ofsted.

Page, J., & Nutbrown, C. (2008). Working with babies and young children from birth to three. London, UK: Sage.

Pawl, J. (2006). *Concepts for Care: Being held in another's mind*. Available at www.wested.org/ online_pubs/ccfs-06–01-chapter1.pdf (accessed 3 February 2012).

Perry, B., & Dockett, S. (2007). Children's Transition to School: changing expectations. In A. Dunlop & H. Fabian (Eds.), *Informing transitions in the early years: Research, policy and practice*. Maidenhead, UK: Open University Press.

Plotsky P. M., Owens, M. J., & Nemeroff, C. B. (1998). Psychoneuroendocrinology of depression: Hypothalamic–pituitary–adrenal axis. *Psychiatric Clinics of North America*, *21*, 293–307.

Pre-School Learning Alliance. (undated). *Our history*. Available at www.pre-school.org.uk/ about-us/history (accessed 5 February 2012).

Read, V. (2010). Developing attachment in early years settings. London, UK: David Fulton.

Registered Childminding. (2010). *The history of childminding*. Available at www.childminding-success.co.uk/business/history-of-childminding (accessed 13 February 2012).

Robinson, M. (2003). *From birth to one: The year of opportunity*. Buckingham, UK: Open University Press

Robinson, M. (2011). *Understanding behaviour and development in early childhood: A guide to theory and practice*. London, UK: Routledge.

Sanchez, M. M., Ladd, C. O., & Plotsky, P. M. (2001). Early adverse experience as a developmental risk factor for later psychopathology: Evidence from rodent and primate models. *Development and Psychopathology*, *13*, 419–449.

Sanders, D., White, G., Burge, B., Sharp, C., Eames, A., McEune, R., & Grayson, H. (2005). *A study of the transition from the foundation stage to key stage 1*. London, UK: DfES.

Sansom, C. (2004). *Summary of 'Transition to child care: Associations with infant–mother attachment, infant negative emotion, and cortisol elevation by Ahnert et al.'*. Available at www.whataboutthe children.org.uk/images/stories/PDF's/Transitionintochildcarepdf09.pdf (accessed 29 May 2012).

Schore, A. (1994). *Affect regulation and the origin of the self*. Hillsdale, NJ: Lawrence Erlbaum Associates.

Schore, A. (2001). Effects of a secure attachment relationship on right brain development, affect regulation and infant mental health. *Infant Mental Health Journal*, *22*, 7–66.

Selleck, D. Y. (2006). Key persons in the Early Years Foundation Stage. *Early Education*, no. 50, Autumn.

Selleck, D. Y. (2009). The key persons approach in reception classes. *Early Education*, no. 57, Spring.

Sharp, C., George, N., Sargent, C., O'Donnell, S., & Heron, M. (2009). *International thematic probe: The influence of relative age on learner attainment and development.* Slough, UK: NFER. Available at www.nfer.ac.uk/nfer/publications/QSB01 (accessed 15 March 2010).

Shields, P. (2009). 'School doesn't feel as much of a partnership': Parents' perceptions of their children's transition from nursery school to reception class. *Early Years, 29*, 237–248.

Siegal, D. J. (1999). *The developing mind: Towards a neurobiology of interpersonal experience.* New York, NY: Guilford Press.

Stam, R., Akkermans, L. M., & Wiegant, V. M. (1997). Trauma and the gut: Interactions between stressful experience and intestinal function. *Gut, 40*, 704–709.

Stormont, M., Beckner, R., Mitchell, B., & Richter, M. (2005). Supporting successful transition to kindergarten: General challenges and specific implications for students with problem behaviour. *Psychology in the Schools, 42*, 765–778.

Sunderland, M. (2006). *The science of parenting.* London, UK: Dorling Kindersley.

Sure Start (2002). *Delivering for children and families: 2002.* Interdepartmental Childcare Review. London, UK. Sure Start.

Szretzer, R. (1964). The origins of compulsory schooling for five year olds. *British Journal of Educational Studies, 13*, Issue 1.

Thomas, S. (2008). Thinking about paired and shared key caring. *Early Education Journal*, No. 54, Spring.

Thorp, M., & Manning Morton, J. (2006). *Key times: A framework for developing high quality provision for children birth to three.* Oxford, UK: Oxford University Press.

Tickell, C. (2011). *The early years: Foundations for life, health and learning.* Available at http://media.education.gov.uk/MediaFiles/B/1/5/%7BB15EFF0D-A4DF-4294–93A1–1E1B8 8C13F68%7DTickell%20review.pdf (accessed 28 May 2012).

Tizard, B., & Hughes, M. (1984). *Young children learning.* London, UK: Fontana.

Vecchi, V., & Strozzi, P. (Eds.). (2002). *Advisories.* Reggio Emilia, Italy: Reggio Children.

Wells, G. (1985). *The meaning makers.* London, UK: Hodder and Stoughton.

Whalen, P. J. (2007). The uncertainty of it all. *Trends in Cognitive Sciences, 11*, 499–500.

Whitbread, N. (1972). *The evolution of the nursery–infant school: A history of infant and nursery education in Britain 1800–1970.* London, UK: Routledge and Kegan Paul.

Winnicott, D. (1953). Transitional objects and transitional phenomena. *International Journal of Psychoanalysis, 34*, 89–97.

Winnicott, D. W. (1965). *The maturation process and the facilitating environment.* London, UK: Karnac.

Working with Men (2004). *Willpower challenge.* London, UK: Working with Men.

Websites

- What About the Children? www.whataboutthechildren.org.uk

- Early Education: www.early-education.org.uk

- Siren Films: www.sirenfilms.co.uk

- Nursery World: www.nurseryworld.co.uk

- Pre-school Learning Alliance: www.pre-school.org.uk

- Registered Childminding: www.childminding-success.co.uk

- NCMA: www.ncma.org.uk

- 4Children: www.4children.org.uk

- For information about Reggio Emilia pre-schools: www.sightlines-initiative.com

Index

trauma 7, 71, 73
'travelling key group' 96–7
'triangle of trust and attachments' 77
trust 4, 63, 73, 77
Tutaev, Belle 35

uncertainty 8, 101, 104, 126; emotional
    regulation 3–4; insecure attachment 7;
    parents 102; as a threat 24–5
urbanisation 32, 51

Vecchi, V. 78
vertical grouping 84–8, 98

visits to settings 101
vulnerable children 72–4, 78

Wales 44
welcome packs 101, 110
well-being: attachment 13, 14; belonging
    56; practitioners 76; relationships
    with parents 98; supporting 99–124;
    unrelieved childhood stress 20
What About the Children? (WATCh) 22,
    25, 29
Wilderspin, Samuel 33
Winnicott, Donald 28, 105, 115–16